Learning About Dogs

Clicker Intermediate Training

Kay Laurence

LEVEL

3

CLICKER
TRAINERS
COURSE

Printed in the U.S. and distributed by
Karen Pryor ClickerTraining and Sunshine Books
49 River Street, Waltham, MA 02453
www.clickertraining.com
Sales: U.S. Toll Free 800-472-5425
          781-398-0754

First published in 2004

Learning About Dogs Limited

PO Box 13, Chipping Campden, Glos, GL55 6WX. UK

ISBN 1-890948-25-X

Books in the Clicker Trainers Course series by Kay Laurence:

> Clicker Foundation Trainer Level 1
>
> Clicker Novice Trainer Level 2
>
> Clicker Intermediate Trainer Level 3
>
> Clicker Advanced Trainer Level 4

Recipe books for specialised interests to progress from Level 2

> Clicker World Competition Obedience
>
> Clicker Dances with Dogs
>
> Clicker Ringcraft

Clicker Agility for Fun and Fitness by Diana Bird

Teaching Dogs Magazine for up-to-date news on clicker training

www.learningaboutdogs.com

CONTENTS

1 Introduction

Congratulations on arriving here and a word of caution. You must realise by now that you are hooked by clicker training? Now we move onto the seriously addictive stuff and get deeper into the secret places of clicker training, the true engine of the process.

To get the most benefit from this book you should be confident to:

◆ Repeat a behaviour at least 10 times maintaining motivation, focus and the same standard of quality throughout. Simple behaviours such as the sit, beg or shake a paw.

◆ Use the technique of targeting to acquire a new behaviour and be able to take the target away when the behaviour is put on cue. Such as the spin, touch, paw.

◆ Finish behaviours to a high standard and add either a verbal or visual cue. Examples: a paw by hand signal, or a paw "wave" signal, or a hand signal to beg or the word "beg".

◆ The finished behaviour should maintain the same strength and quality with a one click and one reward (1:1) reinforcement in a range of different venues.

◆ Free shape, no luring of cue hints, a new behaviour that is a stand alone physical movement, perhaps a step sideways, a tucked sit as opposed to a back sit, a head nod.

◆ Free shape a new behaviour that is interaction with an object, example stand on a stool, tap a cone, go around a post.

Make sure you have given yourself plenty of time to develop these skills and acquired them with understanding and fluency. All this training is covered in the Novice Training Course.

You should now be able to take simple behaviours and finish them to a high standard, with the strength in these behaviours to ask for them anywhere, any time and any place.

THE PROCESS IS ALWAYS THE SAME

When teaching every new behaviour the process is the same:

1   MAKE A PLAN

Break down the behaviour into the teaching parts. These are usually the smallest behaviours that we use to enable the dog to understand what we are looking for. It may be as simple as a step towards an object, a glance or a change of balance.

2   GET THE BEHAVIOUR

For each individual behaviour teach to attain the finished quality, the attitude, the fluency and the flexibility in this building process.

This means no hesitation when performing the behaviour after reinforcement, with a keen "let me do it" attitude, and very often whilst still enjoying the last reinforcement!

The dog can perform the behaviour approaching from different locations, over slightly longer distances, past minor distractions and show fluency.

The behaviour is the same quality every time. There is very little variation, and the dog reaches the highest standard again and again.

The dog shows an understanding of what is expected by doing the behaviour with strength.

Use a temporary cue to develop this.

3.   CHANGE TO THE FINAL CUE

This is the cue that will last for the lifetime of this behaviour. You may have used a hand signal during the building process to get the best quality sit, but long term you wish this behaviour to be signal free and only give a verbal cue.

Add the verbal cue after you have completed the building, this means the final cue will be attached to only the best quality behaviour.

If you are free shaping, allow the environment or the object to act as the temporary cue. I usually free shaping only one behaviour at a time, then the free shape set up or situation triggers only that behaviour until it goes on cue.

Get reliability to the new cue. Build up the flexibility of the dog to "find" your cue amongst a host of different stimuli - a movement may be distracting, a noise, a scent or another dog. Every new location is a plethora of distractions.

At this time check that if the behaviour is not cued is DOES NOT HAPPEN.

4. ADD TO YOUR TRAINING SESSIONS

Take this new behaviour into practice sessions with other behaviours.

Build to last a lifetime, build for unexpected bad weather and allow for future expansion plans.

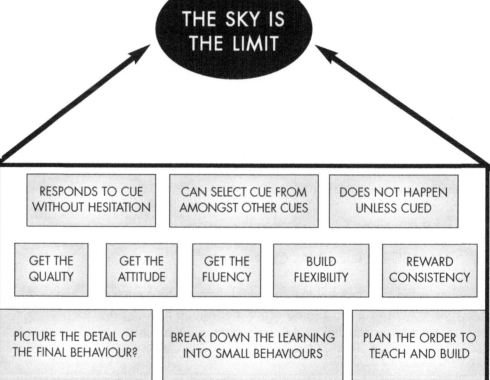

4	Add to the training
3	Change to the final cue
2	Get the Behaviour
1	Make a plan

THE SKY IS THE LIMIT

| RESPONDS TO CUE WITHOUT HESITATION | CAN SELECT CUE FROM AMONGST OTHER CUES | DOES NOT HAPPEN UNLESS CUED |

| GET THE QUALITY | GET THE ATTITUDE | GET THE FLUENCY | BUILD FLEXIBILITY | REWARD CONSISTENCY |

| PICTURE THE DETAIL OF THE FINAL BEHAVIOUR? | BREAK DOWN THE LEARNING INTO SMALL BEHAVIOURS | PLAN THE ORDER TO TEACH AND BUILD |

STRENGTH IS FLEXIBILITY

To ensure a behaviour has strength you need to build flexibility into the behaviour. This will give the dog a deeper understanding of the behaviour and result in a stronger behaviour.

Take the retrieve. This is a complex sequence of behaviours. Each behaviour is taught individually and put together to make a whole exercise. Your dog may only need to collect and retrieve a certain type of object, but by teaching retrieve on a range of objects the dog will have a stronger understanding of the essence of retrieve. Some of the objects will tax the dog's skills to pick up, some will test the dog's ability to carry or even mark where they land when thrown.

Take the jump. If your dog is only expected to jump competition hurdles you still need to train on a range of unexpected jumps to build flexibility: over logs, ropes, low brick walls etc.

Take the recall. On most occasions the recall is a predictable behaviour happening in regular situations. But situations may occur unexpectedly, and in preparation for that emergency situation you need to build the recall in many different places, sometimes when it is least expected. Add flexibility to a behaviour by changing yourself. Try training holding an umbrella, certainly holding a video camera changes a dog's behaviour, recall the dog from a lounger, from one room to another.

The more behaviours we teach a dog, the stronger our teaching skills will become. The more dogs we teach a range of behaviours the stronger our teaching skills become. By adding flexibility in WHAT we teach and to WHOM we teach it, our teaching skills are practised. They become more flexible and adaptable, the process to achieve a higher standard becomes easier and our understanding of the process deepens.

Flexibility builds strength. Strength is flexibility.

If a behaviour is inflexible it will only happen when the conditions are perfect and a small amount of stress will break the behaviour.

2 Teaching and Training

Teaching
session

Training
session

Light training
session

TEACHING AND TRAINING SESSIONS

I differentiate between a lesson for the dog that is the acquisition of a new behaviour - A Teaching Session - and the repetition of established behaviours to maintain strength and fluency - A Training Session.

Each session is approximately 10 minutes. I make a plan for this session and the dog is working hard with only breaks to re-stock with food. I cannot foresee when the dog would have to maintain that level of focus in a working situation for longer than 10 minutes. Some working dogs may work for very long periods but their focus is less intense.

There may be more than one session per day prior to high levels of performance. There may be rest periods when the competition season finishes with only one or two sessions a week.

I do not mix a teaching session with a training session. I find the teaching sessions can mentally tire the dogs more than a training session. I also include mentally "light" training sessions where the dog does not have to mentally engage, but just follow the lure, play games and develop muscle strength and physical flexibility.

I plan to teach or train each dog approximately 5 times a week. They will also get some group training and plenty of ad hoc training through the day's routine, a sit and wait at a gate, a standing still for grooming, a kiss because you're so handsome.

Depending on what your ambitions are, or the time of year, or the age of the dog, you should plan a profile of your lessons. This is the dog's curriculum. The balance between teaching and training needs to suit the individual needs of each dog.

For an athlete or performance dog it is better to build to a peak performance period, rather than maintain a steady standard. All dogs need rest and holidays as much as they need games and fun.

The profile of the week's sessions can be arranged in any order. If the weather is good I may give the dog a good physical work out and build muscle development with jumping or toy games. If the weather is foul we will be tucked up in the kitchen for some shaping.

I only teach one new behaviour at a time. Very few behaviours take more than 5 shaping sessions (see Chapter 7 for Micro Shaping). If I am feeling uninspired I will run a training session.

SEASONAL PLAN

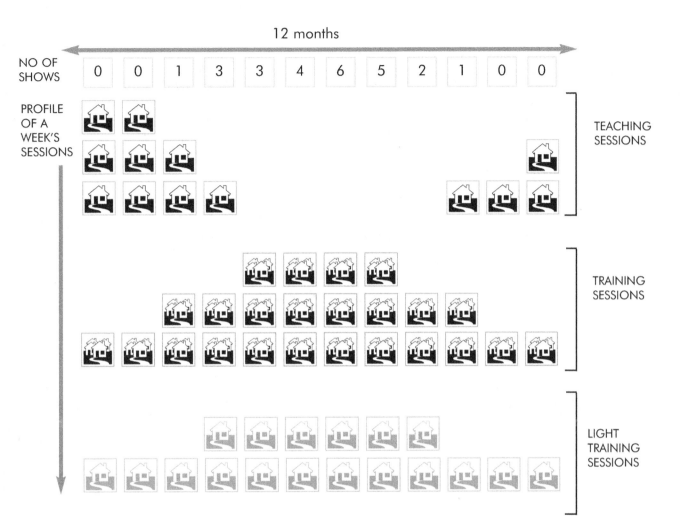

12 months											

NO OF SHOWS

0	0	1	3	3	4	6	5	2	1	0	0

PROFILE OF A WEEK'S SESSIONS

TEACHING SESSIONS

TRAINING SESSIONS

LIGHT TRAINING SESSIONS

For this performance dog the peak is mid summer. The training sessions do not begin in earnest until the teaching sessions are almost completed.

During the off season the training sessions are mostly to refresh the cues to the behaviours. The dog gets a rest period at the end of the season and enjoys learning new behaviours to sharpen the mind before a fresh season starts. No new behaviours are worked on during the performance months.

A PUPPY PLAN
2 - 9 MONTHS

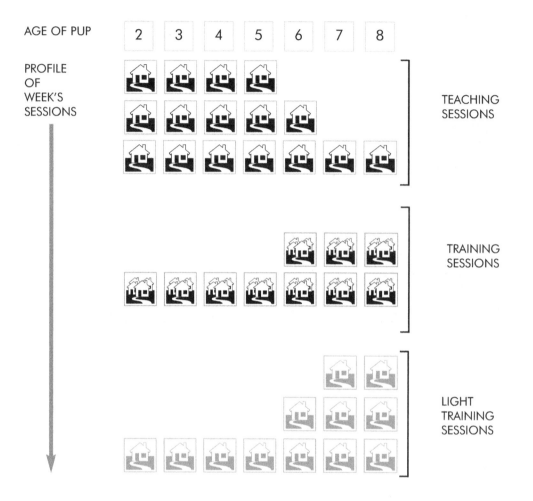

This plan is for 18 new behaviours to be put on cue before 9 months old (anticipating the onset of full puberty and loss of all motor and memory skills). You see the expectation of learning new behaviours reduces after 6 months old. This will pick up again at about 18 months and not slow down until you let it!

The physical training begins to build and is the majority of my expectations at 9 months old.

Establishing training disciplines in the youngster will lay down the foundations for the active mind and teach the dog to focus and develop memory skills. Although they may be some time before any performance or work requirements, learning to train is a performance itself.

You may need to review your training and teachings sessions and see what sort of profile they make.

It is quite likely that if you prefer to teach new behaviours you will see an imbalance in relation to the physical development and training sessions. Do be careful you do not impose your teaching preferences over the dog's needs.

These plans should only be a guide to what your proportion of teaching to training to physical practice is. Take into consideration the growing rate of dogs, their developmental progress, injury time, and your very busy lifestyle!

Keeping a balance between all three types of sessions leads to contented dogs, happy households and a top quality relationship you both enjoy.

At this level the course will expect you to plan your own teaching and training sessions, not only what type of session but what to include in each session. The planning process will give you a clear set of goals to progress towards, a format to measure progress against and you will waste less time.

I personally find it easier to invest time in a plan, rather than wonder what to train with each dog each session. Far easier to refer to the plan and start straight in. Large pieces of paper with post-it notes come in very handy!

A TEACHING SESSION

All dogs need teaching sessions. This is where they learn to learn, develop their thinking and memory skills. It also helps you read the personality of the dog, understand what games they like to play and measure their mental capacities. How long can they concentrate, how many un-clicked behaviour will they try before they give up?

It is particularly useful for a new dog or pup, for developing stressed dogs or lifting the depressed dog. Your expectations of each session can make the dog feel like a hero, or a failure. So regard the long term benefit of each session as a priority, not getting the behaviour perfect just now. Focus on the progress the dog has made. This is much easier to see once you begin to collect data and can see the change in their learning. (This is covered in Chapter 4 Measuring Behaviour).

Some teaching sessions will be pure free shaping. You take your chair, sit back and follow the dog with the guidance of success towards your end behaviour.

Other sessions may be teaching the dog to link two behaviours together or taking two behaviours apart. The key to teaching sessions is the acquisition of something new, perhaps a new concept, like adding cues, or making chains, or a sequence of 5 behaviours without a click. Always place the "new" learning in the teaching session. The element of newness will slow the dog. Here they can take their time, they are trying to learn, the pace of the lesson is to suit the dog.

A TRAINING SESSION

A training or practice session takes the dog through lots of repetitions of known behaviours. Here they develop full working or emergency fluency and the behaviours move from the cognitive zone to the conditioned zone. Just as you learn to touch type or play a musical instrument, there comes a point where you do not have to think where to place your fingers or what note you are reading. The information coming in skips the brain and goes straight to the action. The information "coming in" is the cue, and the dog reacts with the correct behaviour without cognitive process. It would not matter what the behaviour is, a guiding dog stopping at a kerb, or an agility dog turning left on cue, or a dog jumping into the car, all behaviour need to go to this point.

For the majority of the time the behaviours will be rewarded on a high frequency. Without regular rewards even conditioned behaviours will fade. We use the practice sessions to add petrol to the low frequency reward situations, such as work or competition, without which the behaviours would deteriorate. The dog believes the reward is only around the next corner, only after the next behaviour.

With sufficient reward association a behaviour can become self rewarding, which becomes a useful tool in working situations.

I divide the training sessions into:

MEMORY PRACTICE

FIND THE CUE GAMES

HERE AND NOW? MOMENTS

MEMORY PRACTICE covers the majority of the sessions the dog will need lots and lots of opportunities to remember which behaviour goes with which cue. "Aw, come on now, what was the bend?" Remember, a dog cannot check in with their buddy in the next seat. This is similar to acquiring new language skills or increasing your vocabulary. If you do not employ a word with regularity you will forget exactly what it means.

FIND THE CUE is the challenge to the dog to block out all the distractions and look for the cue: "What's coming? .... There it is, here's the bend. Got it!" Often our cues are unintentionally disguised by a distracting movement from the hands, the hint of another behaviour, by a similar tone of a verbal cue, or even contrary cues, where the hands say one behaviour but the voice says another. Which does the dog listen to?

It is a high level skill to employ keen observation and memory at the same time. Rather like hunting I suppose! "Where did they run to last time, and what did they do just before they bolted?" (... and who has just pee'ed on THAT tree?).

"WHAT, HERE AND NOW?" MOMENTS are the integration of the behaviour into the non-training situations. The training and teaching sessions are in your optimum environment for learning and practise. As the training progresses you will find new venues to train in, but each session will have the familiarity of "a training session". This will help the dog focus and tighten their skills and responses, but to add flexibility to these skills calls for the behaviours at odd moments.

Just one behaviour, just once, probably rewarded by the situation. A bow, before the garden door opens. A paw wave before the lead is attached. A beg before a grooming session. Once a behaviour has been moved out of training into every day occurrences you will be surprised at the strength of that behaviour, particularly if you can measure the strength with regular assessment.

For dogs that live in their working environment full time, the training sessions need to be longer and less intense. Consequently the dog's focus is likely to be more reduced and take more than a couple of seconds to respond or anticipate a cue.

TRAINING GAME 1

CAN YOU REMEMBER A ...?

The task of learning new words or cues in association with a behaviour is just as hard as learning the Latin word for "basket", or "fish", or "behaviour" (no, don't ask me!). You learn it one day, but without regular use it will be gone in 2 days. We need to provide fun situations that both of us enjoy to practise these associations. I like to see this as a challenge for "Bet you can't remember which way a spin goes ... ?" rather than an order to "Do the spin". As soon as the dog tells you of course they can remember it by showing you, THAT click gets an extra boost with your congratulations body language.

The timing of this "memory" click is slightly different from just clicking the behaviour. I click the opening of the behaviour, that is, just as the dog has processed the word and gone straight to the correct answer. If it was a spin or a turn and I waited until the turn was nearly complete before the click, the moment of remembering is not getting the strongest reinforcement.

Sometimes this early click can stop the progress of the behaviour, ie the dog will stop when they hear the click and not complete it, but you can continue the cue, or next time withhold the click until the usual moment. I think the possible introduction of some hesitancy is worth being able to say "what an excellent memory". This is the part that often needs strengthening.

It may be the time to introduce a less powerful reinforcer - such as a verbal "great!" or "smart!" and leave the click until the usual time. Pick a single syllable word that easily conveys the intent.

> ▶ Begin the game with selecting at least three behaviours. For the first level choose behaviours that are compatible and start from the same opening position. From the standing in front of you position, the behaviours can be:

from the stand:	**SIT**
from the stand:	**PAW**
from the stand:	**DROP**

Or from the sitting position:

from the sit:	**STAND**
from the sit:	**BEG**
from the sit:	**LIE DOWN**

These behaviours are compatible emotionally and physically. None require high energy and are completed within a second.

▶ Practice each behaviour five times in a row, click and rewarding each one. This is also your final check that each behaviour is maintaining a good quality and consistent standard.

▶ Rotate randomly around the behaviours in batches of 10. Sometimes repeat one twice. You always need to practise memory skills in three or more. If the dog has a choice of only two behaviours, then as soon as they realise they are not right, (no click) they switch to the other behaviour. This is not a memory test! This develops a "try the other one" skill. Be careful you do not reward the dog after a string of errors. Maybe once or twice, but getting it right first time is what earns the click, NOT trying everything until you hit the button.

▶ Build up the number of behaviours to 5 in your group. This will be good practice for you as well as the dog, to keep you cues clean, minimal and consistent.

This game puts an end to the dog offering their complete repertoire until they hit the right behaviour. Naughty trainer! You should have put those behaviours securely on cue, and also put them on "no cue, no behaviour!!!" (Don't worry, most trainers have been down this avenue).

▶ Once the dog can rotate amongst five similar behaviours, go back to 3 behaviours and choose from a less compatible collection. Perhaps add a jump or a bark. A behaviour that excites the dog. By asking the dog to change between high energy - low energy, we are extending their self control and abilities to focus.

from the stand in front (top), the bow, the sit, the right paw

TRAINING GAME 2

PUTTING THE EARS ON YOUR DOG

This is a Welsh expression, rooted in sheepdog training. To successfully work a dog on the sheep they need to be very attentive to listening to your cues whilst watching the sheep, and often running flat out at the same time. A dog that is watching sheep is often "without ears".

▶ To begin with choose a low energy behaviour on a verbal cue. The same behaviours you chose for Training Game 1 will probably be suitable. Set it up so that when you toss the food the dog will turn their back to you to collect, or alternatively move yourself out of visual sight of the dog. Then stand behind them or throw the food behind you. Whilst they are not watching you, give the verbal cue for the behaviour.

This is a test of memory as well. The dog will often have to move back to the opening position, standing in front or the sit in front, before they offer the behaviour.

All behaviours that the dog needs to carry out without direct visual contact should go through this game in practice. All jumping cues, redirection if the dog is facing away, the cue to drop at a distance on the sendaway (the dog is not facing you), if the dog is in another room, with its head down a rabbit hole, and most cues in the heel position since the dog cannot directly see you.

▶ Increase the difficulty by throwing the food further away so that the dog will have a longer time gap between hearing the cue and carrying out the behaviour. This is not the time to expect the dog to carry out the behaviour at the location they hear the cue - this is a merged behaviour (location + behaviour).

▶ Increase difficulty again by choosing food that takes more than a couple of seconds to chew. This is an excellent multi-tasking practice game, especially for dogs who focus deeply on the eating process. Good for future distraction work.

All these variations to teaching the dog to pay attention to the verbal cue add flexibility to this skill. The day you need the dog to hear that cue may be an emergency situation or circumstances you cannot anticipate. Giving the dog lots of experience hearing (and also seeing) their cues will pay dividends in reliability. We know we can teach the dog an extensive range of top quality behaviours, but without reliability to cue it is all a waste of time.

Quiz playing on the tug toy, strengthening her back and her thigh muscles which all contribute to her flexibility and strength for the sit, or high walking exercises, and heads up heelwork.

LIGHT TRAINING SESSION

You are responsible for planning a balanced curriculum for your dog. This will incorporate different types of learning, experiences, mental development, memory tests and physical development.

Strengthening for the side stepping movement

A simple move can be performed with much more ease and fluency if the dog is fit and has had plenty of opportunity to develop the particular fine muscles required for the movement.

For example the dog moving from the down position to the sit. It seems a straightforward movement, but for the dog to perform it with ease they will need physical development.

Strengthening for the walking backwards.

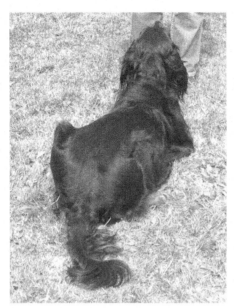

far left - the "lion" or upright down.

left - the rolled or settled down

to move the dog from settle to upright lure the dog forward until the hips come upright and click and reward

If the dog is lying down in the hip rolled relaxed position, the "settle "down, then to rise quickly into a sit is far harder than if the dog is maintaining a lion or sphinx down.

They are BOTH different behaviours and if you wish to differentiate between them they deserve different cues.

The "lion" down is the fast drop, where the dog's spine stays level to the ground, the dog holds the position whilst lying down and is ready for action.

The "settle" down is a more relaxed comfortable position and the dog will not be asked to move at speed from this position. I always reinforce the settle down in the actual behaviour. A click in

To move from upright to a settled position drop the food by the dog's flank and their hips usually roll (click) as they turn to collect the food.

the settle is followed by delivery of the food TO the dog, or a fuss whilst down.

If you watch the dog's hips in the sit, settled down and drop down, you will see that the hips are almost the same in the drop down and sit, but quite different for the settle.

Physical development must be done gradually without ever risking strain to the muscles. If you have a throw-yourself-around type of dog, you need to be more vigilant that their muscles, particularly the small fine muscles, develop their flexibility and strength with care.

Always start from observing the dog's natural movement. Kent makes the decision on how he will position himself in the down before he begins the action. From standing he moves one back leg out sideways about six inches, then tucks the other back leg under to lie down in the settled position. Other dogs may drop and then roll their hips into the settled position after dropping.

The natural movement, the order in which they move what they move, the speed of the movement, the stimulus that causes the movement all need to be noted. You must begin physical development from this baseline, which is individual to each dog. Their conformation, age and structure affect their movements and development potential.

Try an exercise yourself so that you can understand how small amounts of physical movement on a daily basis will improve mobility. Try step training. This is one step up and one step down, change the leading leg half way through. I use the bottom step of the staircase. The first time try 50 of each leg leading, and take a note at what point you either become breathless or your legs begins to ache. Write it down. Over the next 14 days repeat the same number of repetitions and see if the point at which your legs ache gets later and later. This is a small(ish) movement that can really improve your fine muscles in the joints.

If a step is too large to begin with a book or plank, and increase the height of the step after you can comfortably perform 100 repetitions on each leading leg with no muscle aching.

You will also understand why I call this light training. It does not require any mental involvement except for the counting. But this can be looked after by stepping in time to some music for a set duration. I usually step train during a particular TV program!

You get the plan?

1. Find the base line to start from

2. Do a small amount every day

3. Increase the quantity of the easy movement - this is building flexibility and mobility

4. Increase the degree of movement - this build the strength and duration

It is the same plan for canine muscle as for human muscle, BUT young muscle should not go through Step 4 - the strength building movements. Growing must have finished before you begin those exercises.

THE TOASTER - POP UP!

TRAINING GAME 3

This is a great game to teach and a perfect indoor game. If you can, video or take careful note of your dog in the down position and then watch how the dog moves to the sitting position in training. Come back to review the difference after a couple of weeks physical development.

▶ Firstly the dog needs to be able to maintain a lion down position, the "drop".

Lure the dog into the position from standing and click and reward the dog for holding their hips in this position. Initially just maintaining the position for half a second will stretch muscles. Over the next 12 sessions gradually increase the time between the clicks until you can count to ten and the dog holds the position. Any sort of rocking or fidgeting may be an indication of discomfort, take a note, step back on your time count and build more slowly.

Next you must think of the way you want the dog to rise to the sit. I like the dog to use both front legs with equal power and pop in one clean movement rather than alternate the legs and push the upper body into the sit.

The clean "pop-up" requires strong muscles in the dog's hips and back to pull the dog up. I would also teach the dog the beg position to strengthen the back and hips.

luring for the very upright sit, almost the beg

To develop the muscles required I break the behaviour down to the smallest movements:

▶ From the sit position using a target, ask the dog to touch by pointing their head upwards.

▶ Increase the angle of the touch so that the dog's head tips further backwards and the front legs are hardly touching the ground. Don't try and go all the way to the beg position. Just ask for the stretched "moon watching". 10 repetitions every day for 12 days.

▶ In the standing position play a game where you toss the food to the dog and they give a very small jump off the front legs to catch the food. Experiment with over arm and under arm tosses, some dogs can catch more easily one way or the other. An ideal slow moving piece of food is un-flavoured popcorn.

▶ Now ask the dog to start from the sit, catch and return to the sit for the next click. If your throw takes the dog out of the sit, try not to cue the dog, but click if they offer the sit. We are looking for the sit-jump-sit.

a finished "sitting tall" - notice how close his front feet are to his back feet.

▶ The final movement you are looking for will require the dog "jump" out of the down into the sit. I use a hand signal rather like aiming to throw a dart. The Gordons have big mouths but very poor mouth to eye co-ordination (I would hate to see them try a spoon or fork!). The aiming signal is easy for them to anticipate and a great temporary signal until the behaviour is fluent, strong, consistent quality and ready to take on the verbal cue.

Surprisingly, Quiz, hates to catch food, and I use a fast target appearance for this behaviour. She will jump from standing to pop the target stick.

▶ At this point the dog is just learning to catch, by jumping from the down position to a sit. This is physical development only. Once the dog moves smoothly and fluently, add your verbal cue BEFORE the hand signal, and when the dog anticipates the "pop", click and then toss the food for the catch, which is now the sit position.

Initially we use a stimulus (toss and catch) to develop the muscles. We finish with a final cue to trigger the movement, which was clicked on movement and food given in the final position. Perfect.

Luring, target sticks, toys and games are wonderful ways to develop physical abilities without the mental pressures required of formal training. Lots can be achieved with association.

When the dog is working in the cognitive zone, ie "understand and remember" the behaviours, they will respond without any stress if their physical development has been completed before the teaching stage.

If I go back to the analogy of house building. You want a sound building, that is well-built, top quality finish and able to stand up to whatever your weather can throw at it. The house is full of lots of materials and skills. You learn the individual skills before you start on the house. Learn to carry weight before you lug bricks up to the higher walls. The process of building should be a joint project, plenty of fun and guarantee a world of learning along the way.

Preparation and good planning are always good investments.

3 Groups of Behaviours

Behaviours seem to become more complex the more we examine them in detail. A sit used seem a simple sit, but now we know it can be carried out in several different ways, often affected by the behaviour before and after. Not only can the action "to sit" be carried out with variation (back legs collect to front legs, front legs walk back to back legs, one leg tucks under, sit from standing is a different action to sit from lying down) but the position of the sit itself can be in different postures with different attitudes, either ready for action or just to watch the birds fly past. We also have to make the decision whether the variation can be tolerated or not. Unspecific variation adds confusion and ambiguity. Not so simple any more!

This is the core of learning to communicate in a language of behaviours to an animal. We need to break down everything to the point at which understanding is easy for the dog, we are very clear and the behaviour is unambiguous. The second part it to attach a cue to be able to communicate this exact behaviour.

From an uneducated view these behaviours seem simple just as once we regarded the retrieve as "just a behaviour". We can now see it is several behaviours, some of which happen simultaneously and some of which happen one after the other. In order to teach a group of behaviours we use different strategies to join the simple behaviours together.

Behaviours that happen at the same time are referred to as "merged" behaviours. Examples:

▶ Jumping over a hurdle whilst carrying an article

▶ Maintaining a stay position whilst marking a dropping bird

▶ Holding an article whilst moving into the present position

▶ Sitting in the beg position whilst balancing a biscuit on the nose

▶ Listening to the handler whilst ignoring the other dogs

If we add the foundation behaviours of paying attention and watching or listening to the handler, we can see that most behaviours are at the minumum merged with concentration. This is the reason many behaviours can fall apart - the underlying behaviours of focusing or concentration have been lost, or unsuccessfully merged with the other behaviour.

Quite obviously it is easier for both student and teacher to learn the individual behaviours before adding them together. When anticipating future merged behaviours it is good planning to teach one behaviour with a visual signal, another behaviour with a verbal signal then merging the two cues will result in the merge of the behaviours.

Behaviours that happen one after the other, or where the same behaviour is repeated over and over again, are referred to as sequences or chains.

The individual behaviour can be cued directly by you:

Examples:

- ▶ Agility course: jump, left, jump, turn, chute, tyre, table

- ▶ Freestyle: spin, turn, walk back, spin, bend, walk back

- ▶ Obedience: stand, sit, down, stand, drop, hup

- ▶ Sheep Dog: runout left, stop, walk on, stop, turn right, stop

Or the can be indirectly cued: by familiarity of repetition, the environment or other objects.

Examples:

> Indication sequence: started with "go search", the scent cue triggers the dog to indicate to handler

> Retrieve: the dog runs out on cue from the handler, collects article, turn and runs to the present position without further cues from the handler.

> Put the chickens to bed: the dog goes around the yard collecting the hens, herds them towards their pen and drops once they are in their house.

> Going for a walk: The sequence begins with the opening of the cupboard under the stairs where the coats are stored. The dog jumps up and down barking then moves to the back door, sits looking at the handle.

> Feeding time: a certain theme for a news program triggers the "time of day". The dogs move to their feeding spots in the kitchen and hold the position whilst their dinner is prepared.

> Arriving at the park: dog travel in the back of the car to the park. Three turnings before the park the dog starts to become aroused, the car makes particular noises in sequence which trigger the arousal. (I have experimented with different cars, thinking the cue may have been a particular scent that was at this turning, but it was the changing down of gear and the particular way that I make the corner that the dogs had learned - even a different driver did not trigger the arousal, different style I suppose!)

Which ever complex behaviour you are going to put together it is essential to have a clear idea of:

- ▶ the individual behaviours

- ▶ how you will teach them

- ▶ what temporary cue you will use in development

- ▶ how the behaviour will be cued when part of the group

a simple behaviour   a merged behaviour, where more than two behaviours are happening at the same time, simultaneously.

 a sequence of behaviours

"sit"   "paw"   "down"   "sit"   "beg"   "jump"

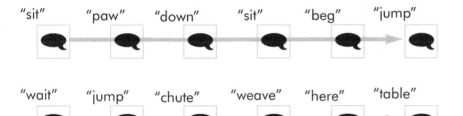

a sequence of behaviours, each directly cued by a signal from you

"wait"   "jump"   "chute"   "weave"   "here"   "table"

a sequence of behaviours, including merged behaviours, indirectly cued

"Fetch" handler's cue releases dog from sitting position	THE DUMBBELL cues dog to run towards and pick it up	HOLDING DUMBBELL cues dog to turn towards handler	THE JUMP cues dog to jump over whilst holding	THE HANDLER standing still in a particular way cues dog to sit in present

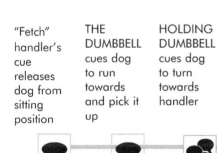

a sequence of behaviours, cued by the equipment

"Over" handler's cue sends dog to A-Frame	THE A-FRAME UPSIDE cues dog make the contact point	THE A-FRAME PEAK cues dog control speed	THE A-FRAME DOWNSIDE cues dog to make contact point	THE HANDLER cues dog to leave contact point

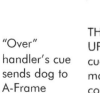

PREPARING BEHAVIOURS

We teach each of the simple behaviours seperately. Individually they may take a variable amount of time for the dog to acquire the strength and skill. But each behaviour must be strong and flexible BEFORE it joins with another behaviour.

For working the dog at a distance from you the behaviour must be strong when close to you, AND the behaviour of "being at a distance" must be equally sound. If the dog lacks confidence at the distance, any behaviour cued at that location will be weakened and distorted:

▶ the sit can turn into a forward movement

▶ the dog will creep forward to lay down or take a step forward when rising to the stand position

▶ the dog will move on the diagonal drawing towards you on redirection instead of staying parallel.

For a retrieve over a jump the dog must be very skilled at retrieving and a strong jumper. When the the behaviours are put together any weakness in either behaviour will be magnified on merging.

▶ If the dog has a poor grip on the article this may be dropped on landing.

▶ If the dog is hesitant in jumping this stress may become evident by an onset of mouthing.

▶ If the dumbbell has landed too close to the jump for a clean return take off, the dog will need the experience, strength and flexibility to clear the jump.

The same magnification of errors will happen in a sequence where a preceeding behaviour can distort the next behaviour.

▶ If the dog races to pick up the article and does not control itself to pick up, the dog will travel through the pick up.

▶ If a dog comes down an A-Frame out of control the contact point will be missed

▶ If a dog is unsure of the presentation sit, the approach to the handler can be slow.

The process for teaching groups of behaviours is exactly the same as every teaching process:

▶ Make a plan

▶ Get the behaviour

▶ Change to final cue

▶ Add to the training session

MAKING THE PLAN

Firstly I describe the behaviour, as if I was giving a full description to a person who has no idea of the behaviour and cannot see it happen.

Retrieve is a great example of a complex behaviour - treat it with the respect it deserves! This is the formal retrieve for competition.

You can leave out the formal stages 1, 2 & 8 if you wish, and have a fun fetch.

BEHAVIOUR - RETRIEVE A DUMBBELL, NO JUMP

1. The dog is sitting by my left side, looking forward

2. As I throw the dumbbell the dog sits still and watches it land

3. On my cue the dog runs out to the dumbbell in a straight line

4. The dog picks up cleanly on first contact, with no running on, or using its feet

5. The dog turns promptly and runs towards me

6. The dog arrives in the sit in front position, perfectly straight in line with my shoulders

7. The dog continues to hold the dumbbell without mouthing until cued to give

8. The dog goes to the heel position and sits, finishes, on my cue

---

Before you turn the page, pick up a pen or marker and make a ring around every verb, or action the dog is to carry out. In the first line you have "sitting" and "looking". Complete the rest of the description yourself.

Next, take a different colour pen or make a line under every location that the dog needs to know. Such as "in front".

You should have picked out 20 words in total. Solution over the page!

GROUP BEHAVIOUR - RETRIEVE A DUMBBELL, NO JUMP

1. The dog is (sitting) by my left side, (looking) forward

2. As I throw the dumbbell the dog (sits) still and (watches) it land

3. On my cue the dog (runs) out to the dumbbell in a straight line

4. The dog (picks up) cleanly on first contact, with no running on, or using its feet

5. The dog (turns) promptly and (runs) towards me

6. The dog (arrives) in the sit in front position, perfectly (straight) in line with my shoulders

7. The dog continues to (hold) the dumbbell without mouthing until cued to (give)

8. The dog (goes) to the heel position and (sits) finishes, on my cue

Take each of these words and list them down the left hand side of the page and write another description of exactly what you mean. How is the dog is to do it? With absolutely no ambiguity, clearly describe it as if you were on the phone to a friend who is not a dog trainer.

Going through this exercise will give you a much clearer idea of what you are teaching.

This is my behaviour list with a description of exactly how I see the dog carrying out the end behaviour.

1.	sitting	this is balanced forward and ready for action
	my left side	the heel position where the dog is facing forwards with their right shoulder level with my left leg. The dog's front feet should be level with the front of my shoes, their rear feet should be directly in line behind their front feet
	looking	the dog will be looking forward ready to watch the dumbbell as it is thrown
2.	sits (still)	as the dumbbell is thrown the dog must not move, whine or fidget

watches   as the dog sits still it must watch the dumbbell all the time

3. *runs (out)*   on my cue, the dog will go straight forwards from the sit at the canter, certainly faster than a trot

    to the dumbbell with no deviation the dog must head in a straight line to the dumbbell and control itself on arrival

4. *picks up*   as the dog arrives it will begin to open its mouth to pick up without hesitation. It will grip the dumbbell on first contact by the centre of the bar

5. *turns*   (this is the crucial bit with a Gordon!) as the dog picks up it will begin to turn back towards me

    runs   whilst gripping the dumbbell the dog must travel in a straight line

    towards me the dog must head for the front of me

6. *arrives*   as the dog arrives it will prepare to sit as close to me as possible without making contact

    in front   I will stand upright and the dog will move into a location directly in front of my hands

    straight in line the dog will sit, with forward balance, with the back feet squarely in line with the front feet. The dog will position itself centred and at right angles to my shoulder line

7. *hold*   the dog will maintain a steady grip on the dumbbell

    give   the dog will release the dumbbell on my cue

8. *goes (to heel)*   the dog moves quickly to the heel position, either around behind me in a clockwise circle to come to heel from the rear, or pivot on its front feet to turn to my left to the heel position

    sit in heel position   as the opening position

The next task is to analyse the cues:

▶   firstly for the final sequence

▶   secondly for the temporary cue you will teach in preparation for the final sequence

This formal retrieve is a collection of 20 behaviours, some of which are merged behaviours. Selected behaviours will be taught before beginning retrieve training, such as the forward sit, the heel position, the recall and the present. When putting all the previously taught and new behaviours together it becomes a very long chain. So this is broken into smaller groups of behaviours that are collected under one cue and then grouped together again.

The first group is the "mark", 1 & 2, the second group is the "pick up", 4, 5, and the third group is the "present", 6 & 7, and the fourth group is the "finish", 8. The links between the first and second group, and the second and third group are the running.

Just looking at the detail of presenting the article (no 6.)

GROUP 3 - THE "PRESENT"

BEHAVIOUR	TEMPORARY CUE	FINAL CUE
6. arrives	"to me" recall with target signal & hand to cue forward sit	target signal hand position target signal hand position
in front	"in front"	standing still with hands in target signal
straight in line	"sit - in front"	standing still with hands in target signal

Dog's skill: running towards the handler, whilst still gripping the dumbbell, able to anticipate the sit and be aware of the location of sitting "straight" as arrives into sit. This is more than multi-tasking!

7. hold	"hold"	the dumbbell itself
give	"give"	the two hands held out to take article

You can see that during teaching there is a temporary cue, which will be adapted to the final cue once the skills (behaviours) are strong and fluent. Retrieve is a complex exercise although some dogs may carry the desire-to-retrieve "genes", they will still need to practise the individual behaviours to acquire them at full strength and with fluency. Clicker training allows us to teach ALL dogs to retrieve.

In Appendix B you will find a collection of groups of behaviours with a chance to practise breaking them down into the skills, actions and locations, working out the teaching and the temporary and final cues. These cover a range of activities for pet, sport and working dogs.

The one element all the groups of behaviours have in common:

▶ they will be completed as a group

▶ they will be reward on completion, not during the sequence

▶ as a group they must flow from one behaviour to another without delay or hesitation

To be able to take the simple behaviours we have taught and put them into groups, either merged or as sequences, we will need to:

▶ ensure each behaviour is strong and maintains strength when in the group

▶ ensure each behaviour can remain strong without reinforcement when in the group

Once you begin to link the behaviours together and the dog is being rewarded at the end of the last behaviour, you may click an individual behaviour, or you may choose to click each behaviour (not advised at this stage).

Whichever way:

▶ some of the behaviours will not be fed

▶ some of the behaviours will not get clicked.

If the behaviour is not completed, or weak, this removal of reinforcement will weaken it further. You will then have a sequence with hesitancy, which may affect the behaviours either side of the weak behaviour.

This is nearly always the cause of a group behaviour falling apart.

To be able to do build groups, we will need additional tools:

▶ to measure the strength of a behaviour so that we can monitor if it is deteriorating or not

▶ to wean the individual behaviours off the reinforcment, either the click or the food or other reward, and keep the strength

▶ teach the dog to anticipate the cues for the fixed sequences and read simultaneous cues for the merged groups

4 Measuring Behaviour

Initially committing behaviour to pen and paper, measuring and analysing it can seem a mountainous task. A behaviour is an action, full of artistry, attitude and skill and these elements are hard to measure, and to some degree take away the breathless awe that a "magic" behaviour can fill us with.

As we build the dogs' repertoire of behaviours and cues the complexity of the lessons increases and it is easy to get bogged down in a "where was I?" situation.

I am regularly teaching 4-5 of my dogs in any one week, they all have different needs and they are all progressing through their behaviours at different rates. I need to have a good paperwork system to keep track of the lesson plans, let alone the individual behaviours.

From designing a system which helped me track progress, I became more focused on progress rather than reaching the end result. I was able to see the dogs acquire more fluency, remember more cues, flip between behaviours without hesitation, it was written down, and I could measure the progress.

Making a habit of measuring behaviour will start to change your perspective and allow you to move on to more advanced teaching techniques.

HOW MANY BEHAVIOURS?

To begin with I teach in batches of 10 behaviours in a row. The dogs seem to enjoy the repetition, and with a break every 10 behaviours, only for 10 - 15 seconds, they are able to do more behaviours than if I asked for 60 behaviours without a break.

How do I know this?

I can measure it.

Beginning with 10 slices of sandwich meat, cut into squares and place near to your hand for counting.

A behaviour needs to have two qualities:

▶ **IT IS FLUENT**
The dog works through the behaviour with no hesitation. Their whole body knows exactly what to do, how to do it, the tail knows where to go, the back legs are in the right place and the face says: "Got it".

▶ **IT IS ON CUE**
The dog can remember the cue and respond with the correct behaviour without a "ooo...errrrm... " moment.

These two together make a behaviour STRONG.

So when measuring a behaviour we measure it by strength, which is the two components - physical skill and memory skill. If the behaviour is lacking strength, you need to identify which area the dog will need more chance to practise.

MEASURING STRENGTH

We measure strength between 1 & 3:

0= the behaviour did not happen at all

1= the behaviour was weak in both memory and physical skill

2= the behaviour was weak in either memory or physical skill

3= the behaviour was strong in both memory and physical skill

When measuring or recording behaviour I work to the same system or grid. I know where the results must go and can spend more time looking at the dog rather than the piece of paper.

I set up the work so that the number of behaviours goes down the left hand side of the page, and the type of behaviour is at the top of the column.

To be able to measure the 60 behaviours without counting, I measure the titbits out in piles of 10. I can reach for each pile without the dog seeing, or I can take a moment to recharge and give the dog a break.

Behaviour:	Sit	Down	Paw
1			
2			
3			
4			
5			
6			
7			
8			
9			
10			

To analyse the durability of the 60 behaviours in: (a) 60 behaviours continuous and
                                                      (b) 60 behaviours break every 10

Dog: Arnold   Age: 3yr   Place: Kitchen

TEST A: 60 BEHAVIOURS CONTINUOUS   Reward ratio: 1:1

Behaviour:	Sit	Down	Paw(L)	Bend	Sleepy	Back
1	3	3	3	3	3	3
2	3	3	3	3	3	2
3	3	3	3	3	0	3
4	2	3	3	2	3	2
5	3	2	3	3	3	2
6	3	2	3	3	3	3
7	3	2	3	3	2	2
8	3	3	3	3	3	3
9	3	2	3	3	3	3
10	3	3	3	3	3	3
% at No.3	90%	60%	100%	90%	80%	60%

TEST B: 60 BEHAVIOURS WITH BREAK EVERY 10   Reward ratio: 1:1

Behaviour:	Sit	Down	Paw(L)	Bend	Sleepy	Back
1	3	3	3	3	3	3
2	3	3	3	3	3	3
3	3	3	3	3	3	3
4	2	3	3	3	2	3
5	3	2	3	3	3	3
6	3	3	3	3	3	3
7	3	3	3	3	3	3
8	3	3	3	3	3	3
9	3	2	3	3	3	3
10	3	3	3	3	3	3
% at No.3	90%	80%	100%	100%	90%	100%

This is the result of Arnold's tests: By measuring the behaviours over the 60 test behaviours I was able to see that the quality was maintained, ie there were just as many "3" in the last 10 as in the first and third, when the dog had a break of 10-15 seconds between each batch of 10.

The dogs were all tested on the same behaviour over the 60 repetitions, and at different times on different behaviours. This was 60 sits, or 60 downs, or 60 paws etc. There is a blank form to copy in Appendix A

From time to time I will run the test again, and the order of the behaviour will change. I tried the test on 2 collies and 2 Gordons, plus dogs at the classes. Out of the 8 dogs we tested, 7 of them performed better, that is they maintained a 100% rate for longer, when the behaviours were cued in batches of 10 with the 10-15 second break in between.

The dogs were allowed to do what they like during the break. Arnold comes over to the food reserve and makes a judgement of how much space is left in his stomach, Mabel likes to rub against me, Quiz will just stand and stare. The only dog that did not show any difference between the batches or the continuous was a competition obedience dog, and I think the training history of this dog was such that he found the extra reserves even when he was tiring.

HOW MANY BEHAVIOURS?

It depends on the dog's ability to maintain over 90% strength 3 behaviours.

If you are trying to increase the dog's training stamina, you will see this increase if your training strategy is effective. (The batches of 10 fast behaviours is also a good stamina building exercise).

If you are trying to build the dog's ability to focus with distractions you will see from the results of your measuring if the dog is increasing or decreasing.

If you are trying to build the dog's physical strength, again you will see at what point the dog tires. If you want to measure physical strength over mental strength, then stay with the same behaviour for the batches of 60 to measure the dog's muscle power. Changing behaviours will use different muscles.

With a dog at full strength for these behaviours it takes approximately 30 seconds for 10 behaviours.

6 batches of 10	=	5 minutes
60 continuous	=	3.5 minutes

Not a lot of your training time to measure and analyse. Your results can then directly relate to how you plan your next session and your time, and the dog's, will be spent more effectively. To begin with it is hard to measure and train, so video your training, measure afterwards or train with other clicker folk. It is great practise to measure lots of different dogs with a range of behaviours.

Before you begin to measure, both you and the trainer must agree the start point of a "Strength 3 Behaviour".

LEARNING TO MEASURE

I have evolved different techniques to be able to measure whilst "on the job". It involves observation skills, where you can quickly make a judgement on the behaviour, was it a strength 2 or a 3? You will also need to learn the data gathering skill of writing without looking at the paper - you sort of develop a knack of keeping the paper in view of the eyes watching the dog.

The place to get these skills up to speed is analysing other dogs during their training, or if you have the Clicker Clips video you will see behaviours repeated and this will give you some practice. By learning to measure on paper you will become more adept at measuring in your batches without paper.

I like to measure for strength when building a behaviour. I will take note of how many are at strength 3, 2, or 1, and quickly analyse what to do to bring the behaviour up to a consistent 3.

If I get more than one strength 1 consecutively, I will stop. It is a fair indication that the dog has lost the behaviour and to continue will only reinforce the lower strength behaviour. Not desired!

If the dog does not respond for any reason, I place that piece of food back on the counter, or in my other hand. (I have started with a counted batch of 10. To measure out 10 pieces, I chop 10 slices of chicken meat or 10 hot dogs in one cut, and move these away in stacks).

WHEN SHOULD I INCREASE THE CRITERIA?

This is a critical question that is part of the grey area called the "art of teaching".

If you increase the criteria too soon you can take the dog out of the confident zone and motivation will dip. Increasing criteria is quite tiring for the learner and not particularly reinforcing. But if you increase the criteria too slowly the dog can begin to get bored and disengage in the puzzle.

I look for at least five consecutive repetitions of the behaviour, at that stage of the learning, that are strength 3.

Perhaps the dog is learning to stand on a stool. To begin with the dog may look at the stool, the next step is to walk towards it, the next step will be to place a paw on the stool. If this is the stage the dog is at, then I will not increase the criteria (change the weight to this foot when on the stool) until the dog has shown me that behaviour five times in a row, each with strength 3. If at any time the dog uses the wrong foot, or hesitates, or misses the stool, I begin the count again.

The consecutive batch of five strength 3 behaviours is a good measure that the dog is mentally secure in what is expected, and the muscles have developed a pattern for the next stage. At this point when you withhold the click, the dog will be a little surprised and very ready to try the next criteria. This is the key point - the dog is ready to move on up.

If you want to experience this yourself, play the Genabacab Game, and ask your teacher to increase criteria quickly. Everything will start to become harder, to concentrate, to think imaginatively and you even doubt what you got the last click for. Often you see people try several behaviours in a row that simply don't get clicked, but they keep on trying them. The opportunity to repeat what YOU think is right, five times in a row, is very motivating and boosts your self confidence for the next part of the puzzle.

If there is an overload of increasing criteria, there is often a reversion to an early stage. If you have built each step with the strength-3-five-repetitions then the learner will just go back to that point if they are overloaded or tired. It acts like an anchor.

This is a good exercise to build into all your teaching and training. Learn to count five behaviours in a row that are perfect at that time in their development. You may be training against a distraction. As soon as the five in a row is secure, then the distraction is no longer a distraction, but is now probably part of the cue for a top quality behaviour.

This same measuring technique can be used to measure:

▶ when the behaviour is ready for the final cue

▶ when to increase the distraction level

From this five in a row training, you will learn to get a feel for "five of the best". Gradually build up to ten behaviours in a row, and take a note of whether there has been a less than "3" behaviour. You can allow for an odd behaviour to fall by the way side, a momentary distraction, a thought of an itch, or a fluffed cue from you, but if you are getting more than a couple of less than strength 3, then time to take a think, step back, and change strategy. Either the situation is not good, the dog is tired, or you may be tired.

CLICK OR NO-CLICK

We all understand that the click means "you are right". It marks what the dog did to earn the subsequent reward. But the grey are of "no-click" can mean:

▶ you are not right, choose something else

   OR

▶ you are not good enough, stay with this but improve it

By securely attaching all new taught behaviours to their cues, we should avoid the first "choose something else". This can be reserved for creative shaping. (See Chapter 7 Micro Shaping and more games).

The second "not good enough" no-click, ie we are selectively clicking for quality, can drain away the dog's confidence if we over no-click.

I would avoid dropping below 70% clicked behaviours for experienced dogs, and not below 90% clicked, successful, behaviours for inexperienced dogs.

To measure the click rate, (the number of clicks per minute, and the ratio of clicks to behaviours offered), is a key skill. To practice this you will need to watch clicker training rather than participate.

▶ You will need a timer, to be able to check one minute's worth of training. Preferably with an audible "time's up".

▶ Take your sheet of paper and number the left hand side 1 - 30.
   I find most dogs can manage between 20 - 30 maximum behaviours in 60 seconds on a 1:1 ratio, ie one click for one reward, (a very rare dog works at the top rate 26-30).

▶ Across the top each column can be headed Behaviour 1, 2, 3, etc.

▶ To mark successful, I use the diagonal line of the tick (/). If a behaviour is offered but NOT clicked I put a second line though this for a cross. (×)

The column of 20 behaviours may look something like this:

When asking someone else to train whilst you practise collecting information, tell them when to start, from the stop watch, and when to end.

Count EVERY behaviour that happens. These are not just the obvious behaviours such as sit, or wave a paw, but the head flick, the fidget, the look out of the room, the lick of lips. Count ALL behaviours.

The quantity of non specific behaviours offered will give you feedback about the dog's level of concentration, these should drop as the dog becomes more focused.

This is a profile of improving the fluency and quality of a sit, over 5 minutes of training with a 1 minute break in between. The food is consistently thrown to the floor between the front feet which causes the dog to stand. A line is drawn across when the 1 minute is up. Kent is rather a clumsy eater and did not exceed 19 sits in one minute at his best rate. Not

behaviour:	1
1	/
2	/
3	/
4	×
5	×
6	×
7	/
8	/
9	/
10	×
11	/
12	×
13	/
14	/
15	×
16	/
17	/
18	/
19	/
20	/

only does the rate of clicks per minute increase (an indication of growing confidence and fluency), but also the rate of success.

To eliminate poor quality sits, I only "no-click" one specific type of poor sit in each lesson.

behaviour:	1	2	3	4	5
1	/	/	/	x	/
2	/	/	/	/	/
3	x	/	/	/	/
4	/	/	/	/	/
5	/	/	/	/	/
6	/	x	/	/	/
7	/	/	x	/	x
8	x	/	/	/	/
9	x	/	/	/	/
10	/	/	/	/	/
11	/	x	/	/	/
12	x	x	/	x	/
13	/	/	/	/	/
14	/	/	/	/	/
15	/	/	/	/	/
16	/	—	x	/	/
17	—		/	/	/
18			/	/	/
19			—	/	/
20				—	—
Rate per minute:	16	15	18	19	19
% of success:	75%	80%	89%	89%	94%

The skills will be key to your ability to observe behaviour in increasingly fine detail and at the same time get a good feeling for the rate of progress.

Dropping the food to the floor just in front of his feet caused the back end to stand, and the front end stays reasonably still. This way he (a bear of little brain) only needs to send messages to his back legs.

This is an essential part of your skills as a teacher: to plan the curriculum for your dog, not only in what they learn, but being able to assess their progress and also evaluate your teaching skills.

I don't recommend you become obsessed about reading figures, but do learn and analyse how progress is being made. It is the comparison of the figures that will give you information, not comparing one dog against another, but the progression one behaviour makes for that dog.

GIVE US FEEDBACK

I can get a little obsessed about data, but this is under control, the Gordons see to that by blowing all data collection out of the window - literally!

It is important in all stages of developing new teaching and training systems that we learn to rely on hard evidence rather than anecdotal evidence.

I have given you an example: "the dogs prefer to train in small batches". This is a personal statement backed up by data collected on 4 of my dogs and 4 dogs that come to my class.

Data collection needs to be thought out before too much reliability is placed on it. Although the data seems to back up my statement there are considerations that can affect the results:

> ▶ do the behaviours selected affect the results?
> if I had chosen a different range of behaviours, that were high or low energy, or more or less self reinforcing for the dog, would the results have been the same?

> ▶ does the order of the behaviours affect the results?
> if the behaviours that were more self reinforcing were towards the end of the batches would the energy levels of the dogs have stayed higher?

> ▶ does my style of teaching affect the results?
> with my experience I may have taught the dogs to be more comfortable working in batches of 10 from an early age, rather than ask them to work for longer without a break
>
> similarly, my style of teaching my students may have an effect on the results.

So in conclusion, to prove my statement:

> "The dogs work for longer at a higher quality if they work in short
> batches of behaviours rather than continuous training"

needs to be proven with many dogs, trained by many different
people, with different training histories and variable orders of the
behaviours.

Let me know!

OTHER EXPERIMENTS

Another experiment you can look at for me is a "jackpot" theory. I
would like to find out if all, many or some dogs are affected by the
feeding of a jackpot.

The theory can be applied during shaping where you pay extra for
effort. If the dog has made a leap through several criteria, or been
stuck at a level and made a sudden break through, you would pay
several pieces of food.

I have my doubts that this is a useful tool. With the number of dogs
we are seeing in the Competency Tests (CAP - see Appendix A), it
has become obvious that if a dog is paid a jackpot for jumping
ahead and make leaps towards an end goal, they often go
completely off track and leap to the wrong goal. Today we are
training a single dog many, many different behaviours. Dogs are
crossing over from work to sport and between sports, competing and
working at different times of the year in different fields. Shaping is a
critical part of teaching, and I know from teaching in the classroom
that a student that constantly jumps ahead to the end of the lesson
can often be wrong, or if they are right they will miss out some crucial
learning steps along the way.

If I was teaching you to serve a tennis ball to a certain point of the
court, getting the ball to the corner of the service area may seem to
be the goal, but the technique that you use is more important whilst
you are learning than getting the ball into the hot zone.

Having trained collies, who have a predisposition to jump ahead, and
Gordon Setters who live more for the moment, it became obvious
that the Gordons, who learned slower, very often had a better
technique as a result. Today I keep the lid on the collies and make

sure they learn technique! Getting over the A-Frame is not important, how you do it is.

If the goal of your shaping exercise is expand the dog's imagination and creativity, the use of jackpots may help the dog to make brave leaps. But the theory also presumes the dogs is able to relate the quantity of food they receive after a click to the behaviour before the click.

How can you prove this?

You need to be able to record data for the same dog in similar situations, to show that after the payment of a jackpot the behaviour exceeded the expectation than if no jackpot was paid.

This is a good data collection exercise - measuring shaping progress is tricky. It is not just about strength of behaviour, the very nature of learning and experimenting implies a steadiness about the attempts.

Perhaps that is an element? Does the behaviour strengthen quickly on repetition? Does the jackpot affect the speed of the behaviour being strengthened?

What is the rate of behaviours offered per minute? If a dog is offering a high rate of behaviours per minute, does that imply a dog with lots of ideas and creativity? What percentage of these behaviours are successful? Does the jackpot increase this?

To measure the use of jackpots we need to look at dogs in all their learning stages. Dogs at different ages, with different learning histories and different trainers. If a theory can be applied across the range of variations then it is starting to stand on its own.

After all a theory is more useful if it can be applied to the majority of dogs, behaviours and trainers rather than a limited few.

Remember that to measure data you must consider:

▶ all the variables that may affect the results

▶ start with a base line you can measure from

▶ use a unit that you can subjectively measure by

Learn to move away from the terms "good" and "better" - these are subjective views.

Rely on the hard data you have collected:

▶ "increased in strength over 10 behaviours"

▶ "was successful for 85% of the behaviours offered"

These terms are measurable and countable.

If you have ideas for worldwide projects and would like to use the trainer resources of our reader network in Teaching Dogs Magazine please get in touch.

5 Weaning off Reinforcement

This seems to be one of the major worries for many people when looking at clicker training. Not only are the dogs performing fabulous behaviours with the clicker, but the trainers seems to be welded to them, to the point of hysteria if their clicker is not handy.

The clicker is only the TOOL, it is the method that you base it on that is successful.

The click marks the behaviours that will be rewarded. Both the click and the reward are the reinforcers.

We need to be positive in our handling of this stage in the process. We don't "get rid of" the clicker, we don't "stop rewarding the dog". From the dog's point of view they will always get clicked and always get rewarded at some point. We just begin to ask them for more behaviours, or work, before that event occurs.

In a competition the dog may be expected to work several minutes, perform maybe 50 behaviours, most of them repeated, heeling, sit, heeling, about turn, heeling, sit etc, before the reinforcement.

For an assistance or service dog, the dog may be collecting a variety of objects or moving objects around the house, with a low reinforcer for a good length of time, such as verbal encouragement.

For some dogs the tasks themselves are reinforcing.

Clicker training has proved to many of us at this stage that we can teach dogs that have never previously been considered "trainable" a great quantity of complex behaviours. Although I have competed with a Gordon Setter in competition obedience, the collies are far more adept and able to work at the higher levels because of their ability to focus for long periods without reward.

I can teach a Gordon Setter the exact behaviour to an identical standard as a collie, but not without frequent reinforcement.

Clicker training needs to move itself beyond just the teaching phase, and prove that dogs that have a clicker history are as able to compete in a compatible field as any other breed. Physical considerations must be taken into account. Agility is a very athletic sport that will reward dogs with certain physiques where the competitions are dog to dog comparative. Just as equally my collies can't find a pheasant in a field of beans unless they fall over it.

This doesn't stop the ambitious trainer showing that a collie can retrieve birds or a Clumber Spaniel win at agility, but these are tall mountains to climb, and eventhe trainer needs to find reward in the process of the teaching, perhaps not in the end goal!

If you find the process of teaching rewarding, you will not find the end result, perhaps a first class retrieve, exceptionally rewarding. But just as equally the end result may be the motivation that keeps you going through the teaching stage, which you find rather a chore, and without a good end result the teaching would seem pointless.

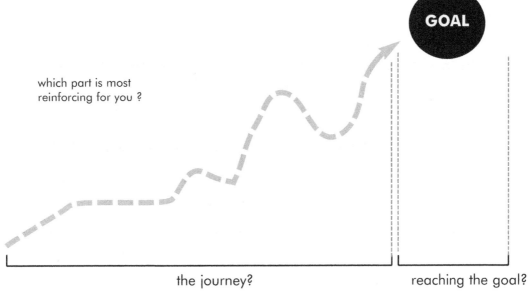

which part is most reinforcing for you ?

GOAL

the journey?   reaching the goal?

For dogs it is the same.

The process of doing the job may or may not be rewarding. Running a bean field for a Gordon doesn't come below second place on any lists of pleasure, but for a collie there will need to be frequent realisation of an end goal, the reinforcement.

▶ The Gordon finds the journey (the behaviour of hunting) self rewarding and does not require an end goal (of finding a bird). I know this because the Gordons will hunt the same field every day without the success of a find.

▶ The Collie does not find the journey rewarding and will only do the behaviour because their IS an end goal, a reward. And a BIG TIME reward for all that pointless runnning around in a stinky field of beans

One simple answer is to find what journey that particular dog finds self rewarding and only train in that area.

Unfortunately bean fields get ploughed and birds get shot. But I can isolate the hunting behaviour that keeps a Gordon self rewarding and seamlessly interweave it into other behaviours. I can find a game for a collie that is about collection and control of moving stock or balls.

I can merge these self rewarding behaviour into non-rewarding behaviours and condition those behaviours to become self rewarding.

The sit at heel for heelwork, the delivery of the article for a service dog, the barking for a hearing dog, the tracking for a searching dog. All these behaviours are part of a larger job and if they were the points of reinforcement the dog could sustain focus and quality for longer periods, ie a high reinforcement rate.

BUILDING SELF REWARDING BEHAVIOURS

All behaviours should become self rewarding if they are rewarded enough times. I do not like to wash the kitchen floor and will schedule this task only when I have purchased an adequate reward, placed it in the fridge and can anticipate this on completion of the task. A fresh cream chocolate choux bun, with coffee.

Washing the floor is still not rewarding. No matter how many choux buns it still is a chore, and if the reward was absent more than once, I doubt I would wash the floor without some threat of punishment (usually embarrassment of visiting folk. Aw come on! Gordon Setters ...). But if I could turn the process of washing into a self rewarding behaviour it may get done more frequently and stop being a chore.

Adding music, so that I can dance whilst washing. Washing with company so that I can have a conversation and laugh. Washing during a good TV program (this works for the ironing, I save it for a favourite program and I don't mind the ironing now). Instead of the reinforcement coming after the task is finished the reinforcement happens simultaneously. The pleasure from the reinforcing behaviours "washes" (sorry for the pun) over the unpleasant task. The two behaviours become merged.

We can use the same technique with a behaviour in training.

Firstly you need to be able to identify a strong, self rewarding behaviour. This is a behaviour that does not need end of behaviour reinforcement, the process itself has pay-off.

For a border collie we can misinterpret that fetching the ball is reinforcing, but for most collies, watching the ball prior to its escape is the reinforcing part. They like to control stock and prevent movement (escape), they contain the energy. Bringing the ball back allows them to carry on using the eye and controlling the ball. Their behaviour is not so intense during the retrieve as during the anticipation of the throw or kick. To check that this part of the process if self rewarding, only allow that part of happen, ie play with the ball on the floor, and keep pretending to kick the ball past the collie. If the dog stays with the game and will only end when you end, it is a pretty fair assumption that it is self reinforcing.

Play the same game with a Gordon Setter and after 30 seconds they will give up. "If you ain't going to kick it then I ain't going to wait".

But take a pheasant wing and pass it across their nostrils and hide it again and you will have self rewarding focus.

Terriers loves to tug and chase, simulating the ratting instincts. Sight hounds love to race with the wind.

There are some base behaviours common to all dogs that we can utilise such as tug playing, prey chasing, affection, attention, eating etc, but the dogs of more highly bred purpose, ie that are genetically carrying strong instincts, seems to be able to merge those instincts more easily with other behaviours. We cannot ignore the hundred of generations it has often taken to breed specialised dogs. If these dogs were not selected on a self rewarding basis, then the jobs would simply not have been done.

Find your self rewarding behaviour and attach it to a cue, both verbal and visual. Make sure either cue will trigger the behaviour and you then have an opportunity to attach the emotion of that behaviour to another behaviour. The stronger emotion will overcome.

Kent loves to travel with me down to the village in the car. We begin the route through Bunny Alley, then progress onto Pheasant Row. This is along the farm track before we hit the roads. Scent comes flowing into the car giving the journey pure pleasure that his nostrils enjoy, a sort of car hunting experience. Some wicked part of me put this behaviour of scenting for birds and bunnies and watching out of the window on the cue "sheeps". Needless to say during this behaviour he is very alert and still as a rock.

I like to show him, because he is beautiful. I think so. He moves very well and is easy to handle, but is an utter pain at standing still in the line up with other dogs. He fidgets and offers lots of behaviours and this standing part can last 5 minutes. Standing still is hard for him, even grooming is under sufferance and needs plenty of reinforcers.

But just one word "sheeps" and he will go still as a rock. Unfortunately his ears prick up as well, which is not "very Gordon", but we are beginning to get the behaviour more solid.

Two things are happening. I cue him to Stand There, get the feet in the right place, then add on the cue "sheeps", at the same time as doubling my hold on the show lead (he is likely to "see" sheeps in the distance, I don't think!). The behaviour of standing still is reinforced by the word "sheeps" (this is the click), the cue marks the behaviour, and the emotion of standing still is being washed over with the emotion of the "sheeps" behaviour.

I need to regularly refresh "sheeps" with travelling down the drive so that the "sheeps" cue maintains its super charge. In addition I walk to the driveway (Pheasant Row) and ask him to Stand There, whilst he can enjoy the behaviour of "sheeps".

Yep, an obsessed dog trainer, but I enjoy the process of seeing this happen. Fascinating for me. I don't need to have the perfect stand in the ring to be reinforced for my effort. Just as a friend would enjoy cleaning the kitchen floor "because it looks so great as you do it". (Yep, true. Can't get there myself though!)

Training and drive instinct can become merged behaviours with experience. The prey drive for the agility dog, where the drive to chase is merged into the course speed, the tug during heelwork, where the action is happening in a specific location. (Both merges also get the dogs physically fit if handled with careful thought).

A search dog hunting a warehouse can be paired with the emotion of hunting a field for game, an attack dog can be paired with toy tug training, a recall can be paired with prey drive. Dogs that are highly food driven can have the search for food paired with many actions, tracking, jumping, recalls. All these behaviours happen during the search for food that you have set up in your kitchen, every evening for their dinner, "where is it?"

REINFORCER OF GREATEST VALUE

With both the click and the reward reinforcing the behaviour, we need to consider how the dog is going to interpret the lack of either. By taking the click off the behaviour we are communicating the "no-click" message:

> No-click= you are not right, try harder

or if we are shaping:

> No-click= try something else

If I ask a dog for a behaviour in a row and remove the click, the dog could be justified in thinking they needed to try harder, or find something else to do. If we have completed our training process properly the dog will already be trying its hardest, it won't be able to sit any faster or any straighter. So what can this lack of click mean?

We will use the click 3000 times to ensure good quality, excellence of memory, strength of focus. We will need to click 3000 times since those behaviours, quality, memory and focus, happen in milliseconds and the click can pinpoint that moment. A "good boy" will not capture that moment.

This is the danger of constant and consistent reinforcement. Not only will it keep the behaviour top quality, but the animal will become dependent on it. The absence of the reinforcement can be perceived as punishment by the dog.

When playing the Genabacab Game in a workshop, a trainer was trying to get their learner to push the car. After 19 clicks and rewards, the learner was still only touching the car, the finger touching the car varied, and the location of the car varied, but no push was forthcoming. The trainer correctly withheld the click on the next touch. No-click = try something else. For this learner the no-click was interpreted as "touching the car is wrong" and she stopped touching the car altogether. The next 12 behaviours offered were touching other objects on the table with avoidance of the car. She then shut down and stopped offering anything.

For this person the lack of click acted as a punisher.

This can happen with dogs as well. For sensitive dogs, the click begins to represent "you are right, I (the trainer) am happy". This is an important piece of information to a young or unconfident dog.

That follow up with the piece of food is great, but for some dogs it is of less value than "being right".

For the next dog the click is purely a promise of the piece of food that follows.

We have two points of reinforcement, so we do not need to delay both reinforcers at the same time. For some dogs the click is of greater value, for some dogs the food, for some dogs they will both be of equal value.

With our ability to measure the behaviour by its strength we can determine which reinforcer should be withheld longer. The dog will always get reinforced, just that because we are asking for more behaviours before the reinforcement is given, the reinforcer is delayed.

START WITH THE BASE LINE

Before we begin this process we have to consider that some behaviours will be more reinforcing that others. For Kiwi, my collie, she loves behaviours of high action, the spin, the weave, the jump, and finds behaviours of keeping still, such as the bow or wave a paw,

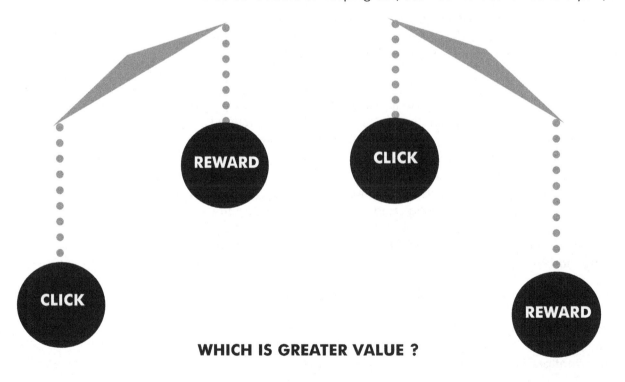

WHICH IS GREATER VALUE ?

much harder to contain herself on. I know this because these are the behaviours that will weaken quickly without regular reinforcers, and if they are part of the sequence they are the first to show stress.

Introducing the "more work before reinforcement" stage is a concept that the dogs seem to transfer between behaviours, just as adding a cue or sustaining a behaviour. Once a concept has been explained on one or maybe two behaviours transferring it seems to be straight-forward. Clicker trained dogs are perceptively bright - don't unestimate what they are learning.

Choose a behaviour the dog enjoys, the behaviour is going to be tested. Choose your premium training area, where the dog is happy to shape and gives you top quality behaviours, a good learning environment with low distraction.

With a second person monitoring and recording the data, ask the dog for 10 repetitions of the behaviour. I chose "spin", and reward 1:1. That is one click for one reward.

IF the 10 behaviours
are 90% at strength 3
you can proceed.

If not,
do not take another step
with this behaviour,
you will only weaken it.

The next step is to click each of the 10 behaviours and do not feed until after number 10 has been completed.

Don't panic, this test is not permanent damage, we are analysing the dog's reinforcer values.

The next step is to no-click but feed after each behaviour.

Your observer will monitor all 30 behaviours. If the behaviours deteriorate completely in either test, only cue the dog a total of three times without result. The dog has taken the lack of click OR feeding as a severe punishment.

When you offer the click, but no food, you may need to re-set the dog as if you had delivered food. If I am testing the sit with Kent, I throw the food to the floor to change the body position to standing, as this allows me to cue the sit again. The alternative is to deliver the food to the dog, and use an interim behaviour after each behaviour to re-stand the dog, touch hand perhaps. Unfortunately the sit is not an ideal test behaviour because of this interim behaviour between the tested behaviours. You can do this with 5 sits and 5 touches alternating. But preferably choose a behaviour that ends at the beginning of the repetition, such as:

> spin or turn

> paw wave (not a sustained high paw)

> tap a target

> weave through one leg

When you do all three tests:

A   the baseline   1:1 ratio

B   the no-click   0:1 ratio

C   the no-reward 1:0 ratio

make sure that the conditions for each are identical. You must stay in the same part of the environment, and hold the clicker and the food exactly the same way for each test.

In the these three tests results we can see that all dogs maintained the strength of the behaviour over the first five repetitions of each test. Their training had been sufficient that the absence of one reinforcer did not start to affect the behaviour until later.

Arnold quickly deteriorated to poor quality when his food was not delivered.

Molly (the collie) began to deteriorate without the click.

Quiz held the same quality with either lack of reinforcer.

TEST: REINFORCER VALUE

Dog: Arnold   Age: 3yr
Location: Kitchen

Test Behaviour: "Blue"
(front left paw wave when standing)

	A 1:1	B 1:0	C 0:1
1	3	3	3
2	3	3	3
3	3	3	3
4	3	3	3
5	3	3	3
6	3	2	3
7	3	2	3
8	3	2	2
9	3	1	3
10	3	1	3

TEST: REINFORCER VALUE

Dog: Quiz   Age: 6yr
Location: Kitchen

Test Behaviour: "Blue"
(front left paw wave when sitting)

	A 1:1	B 1:0	C 0:1
1	3	3	3
2	3	3	3
3	3	3	3
4	3	3	3
5	3	3	3
6	3	2	3
7	3	3	3
8	3	3	2
9	3	3	3
10	3	3	3

On first test Arnold looks like a Food Boy, Mollie is a Click Girl and Quiz is fairly self reinforcing.

There are more tests that can be done, and this test can be questioned:

▶ would it affect the results if the withdrawal of reinforcer was changed around, ie the food withheld before the click?

▶ would it affect the results on different behaviours?

▶ would it affect the results if 6 or 20 repetitions instead of 10 were tested?

I do not want to put dogs through any more testing than is sufficient to find the information. We have tried several of these options and the information gained on the first tests, on the first behaviour, seems to travel through the alternatives with the same pattern.

This minimal test is a quick way to assess your dog and plan how to remover the reinforcer.

TEST: REINFORCER VALUE

Dog: Molly   Age: 2yr
Location: Home

Test Behaviour: "Paw"
(front left paw wave when standing)

	A 1:1	B 1:0	C 0:1
1	3	3	3
2	3	3	3
3	3	3	3
4	3	3	3
5	3	3	3
6	3	3	2
7	3	3	1
8	3	3	2
9	3	2	2
10	3	2	3

We take the least favoured reinforcer away first.

For Arnold, he loses his click, Mollie loses her food, and Quiz loses a roughly equal amount of either.

REMOVING THE REINFORCER

There are two techniques to removing the dog's reliance on either reinforcer:

▶ You can vary which behaviour you click or feed

▶ You can introduce alternative reinforcers

Varying which behaviour to reinforce is a gradual and seemingly random process until the dog stops noticing the absence of the reinforcer.

Of a batch of 10 behaviours (sometimes vary this number to 8 or 12, the dogs are certainly bright enough to feel the end of a batch coming up)

FOR A DOG DEPENDENT ON THE FOOD:

THE BEHAVIOUR:	1	2	3	4	5	6	7	8	9	10
CLICK:	✓	✓		✓			✓		✓	
FEED:	☺	☺	☺	☺	☺	☺	☺	☺	☺	☺

FOR A DOG DEPENDENT ON THE CLICK:

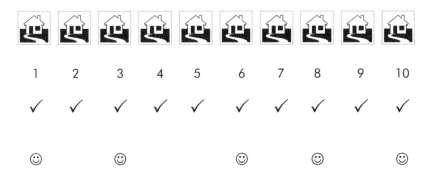

Keep working through batches of 10 until the least important reinforcer is removed and the strength of the behaviour maintains its level
3. This can be done over several days and on different behaviours
that pass the "ten at strength 3" test.

DELAYING THE KEY REINFORCER

The best technique is a mixture of the absent reinforcer and alternative reinforcers, or "half value" reinforcers. Remember this is a
WEANING process and we are teaching the dog the reward will be
delayed.

Alternative Clicks:

▶   tongue click

▶   finger snap

▶   click word

▶   reduced resonance click
     (with the traditional box clicker place your index finger to click
     and your middle finger over the dimple of the metal tongue)

For most dogs these will not have the high impact the traditional
clicker is conditioned to, but still give the dog the feedback they need.
Before employing any alternative except the reduced resonance, you
will need to associate with the traditional clicker, ie tongue click and
feed directly.

The first stage is to replace some of the clicks in your batch with alternatives and the second stage is to remove the traditional clicks altogether.

Alternative food:

▶ the scent of food (pass the food hand under the nose only)

▶ rewarding contact

▶ a self rewarding behaviour, such as jump or spin

The process of delaying the key reinforcer will take longer and should be done more gradually than with the least value reinforcer.

At the end of each batch make sure the dog gets all the reward they need to continue. For the click dependent dog, they will need to have what the click represents, which is a VERY happy trainer, who is THRILLED with their effort.

The food dependent dog, may have several pieces fed one after the other.

At this point you can introduce a more rewarding behaviour that lasts longer, such as a game or good scritching session that may be unsuitable between frequent behaviours.

Every behaviour you wish to group with other behaviours must be able to survive a batch five repetitions with zero reinforcement until completion. We practise in groups of 10 or more but test on 5.

6 Advanced Cues

With your first group of behaviours, plan to build only 3 into one group.

Look through your list of finished behaviours and make a note of which behaviours "complete themselves". Rule out the behaviours that are completed by you cueing another behaviour or the cueing the end. These tend to be behaviours that the dog "keeps going" until a click or cue is given, such as walking back or heeling.

Self Completing Behaviours: sit, bow, down, wave, beg, speak, touch, jump, weave, sleepy.

Place a choice of 5 or 6 behaviours in a circle and draw a line between the behaviours that can connect in the sequence. For instance if the dog is in the sit, and the next behaviour is to be the bow, the dog will have to move into a stand first, so the sit and bow are not behaviours you can link in the sequence.

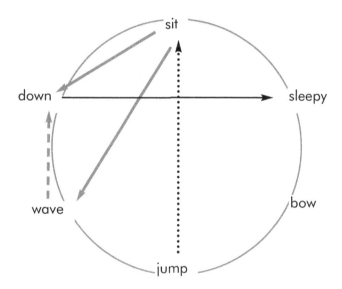

From these behaviours the bow cannot be included since none of these behaviours can link to a bow, sleepy is an "end" behaviour, since we have not included "awake"(!), and jump must be a start behaviour unless the dog can jump out of the down or sit.

A sequence of three of these would be any of:

> jump → sit → wave

or

>> sit → wave → down

or

>>> wave → down → sleepy

When planning a sequence of behaviours do not forget to include your normal default behaviour, which may just be standing in front of you, as part of the chain. The dog will need to include this behaviour to be able to "open" behaviours taught from that position.

Try not to put the dog in the puzzle of being in a standing position when you ask for a "rollover" and having to work out that they need to lay down first.

KEEPING THE SEQUENCE FRESH

Dogs are superb at anticipating, especially repetitions of sequences. This can be to our advantage or a nuisance. The dog that begins to move to the finish as you take the dumbbell, the dog that weaves under one leg and begins to weave the second leg before cued, the dog that leaves the contact point before cue, the dog that knocks you flying when you pick up the car keys. All these are clever dogs being clever.

If you wish to avoid this demonstration of dog-smart, then avoid running the sequence in a predictable order. For the dog that anticipates the finish think of other behaviour you can cue: walk back, spin, beg. Consider the options that you can insert to prevent anticipation.

BUT the other side of the coin is a fixed sequence that we DO want the dogs to anticipate. We call these "self running sequences"

TEACHING A SEQUENCE

A SELF RUNNING SEQUENCE

Plan the sequence of behaviours and begin with just three:

sit → wave → down

If this sequence is is initiated with the cue for the first behaviours we will teach the dog to sit, then give a wave and then lay down without any more cues from you.

Useful, especially if you never want the sit to just be the sit again!

The dog will need information that this sit is the beginning of the self running sequence and not just a sit. To ensure this when planning a sequence you must attach a new opening cue:

STEP 1

"who?" "sit"   "wave" "down"   cues
      sit → wave → down   behaviours

↓
   new cue for the sequence   **(NO CLICK)**
FEED AT END

Repeat this until the dog anticipates the sit, when hearing the cue "who".

STEP 2

Once the "who" is securely attached and has replaced the sit, give the first two cues, and hold your breath before you say the "down". See if the dog is as smart as you think and let them show you they can remember what comes next. Of course they can. As soon as they show you they do not need the cue for the down, click that great demonstration and feed.

"who?"   "wave"   cues
    sit → wave → down   behaviours
             ↓
           click

X 5
FEED AT END

As soon as you have completed 5 repetitions of the 3 behaviours with no cue for the third behaviour and the dog does not hesitate, then drop the cue for the second behaviour.

STEP 3

Now move the click forward in the sequence and click for jumping the gun on the "wave", wait for the down and then feed. If the dog is conditioned to stop the behaviour or sequence on the click, just verbally re-cue the down, and feed after.

"who?"   cues

   sit → wave → down   behaviours
        click

X 5
FEED AT END

STEP 5

The finished sequence will be:

"who?"   sit → wave → down = bucket of food !

One of the traps of sequences is the smart dog syndrome. With this sequence the dog could easily begin to overlap the behaviours.

> The dog could be going into the sit and waving a paw at the same time,

> The dog could be waving a paw as they slide into the down.

If this begins to happen, you will need to introduce an interim behaviour - "wait" between each behaviour making a 5 behaviour sequence.

STEP 8

"who?" "sit" "wait" "wave" "wait" "down"   cues
      sit→wait→ wave→ wait→down   behaviours

If you keep the "wait" time period a consistent gap, the dog will learn the time gap, perhaps count to 2, then cue the next behaviour etc.

This is fun to play with on entertaining routines. If you begin with key words that can begin "questions" then you can adapt the sequence to entertain the onlookers:

> "Who's a plonker?"

> "Who's the smartest?"

> "Who's a hero?"

Other suitable question:

> "What do you think of Scotland?"

This is now Arnold's sequence to drop flat, fall over and raise a back leg. No offence to Scotland, a Gordon Setter IS a Scottish dog! You can obviously substitute any place or person since the cue is "what d'ya think.....?

TEACHING A LONG SEQUENCE

INCREASING THE SEQUENCE

Some of the sequences we will put together may become somewhere between 5 - 10 behaviours. Both people and dogs have difficulty remembering the cues after about 5 in a row, so I put them together in clusters of 3 or 4 until each is fluently on its own cue, and only then put together the whole sequence, with the cue for the last cluster being dropped first.

CLUSTER 1

Cue "Washing Day"

> go out →
> > find my sock in a pile of clothes →
> > > pick it up

CLUSTER 2

Cue "in the basket"

carry the sock →

place in in the basket →

touch nose on bottom of basket
(where there is a target)

CLUSTER 3

Cue "drop dead"

drop into down →

paw over face →

fall over on side

Such fun!

Although the cues of this sequences are initially from you, the dog will be cued by the presence of the objects - the pile of clothes and the basket and these will become the indirect cues. These indirect cues are usually strong and essential elements of a long sequence.

The retrieve becomes the same pattern:

Cluster 1 is the Sit by my Side and Stay and Watch

Cluster 2 is the Go out and Pick up

Cluster 3 is the Recall to me and Sit hold in Front.

Each cluster is taught separately with its own verbal or signal cue and the presence of the dumbbell acts as a cue as well. (For detailed retrieve training and all its variations see the Clicker World Obedience book)

USING A SEQUENCE ON THE SAME BEHAVIOUR

I find this a useful technique to explain to the dog continue the same behaviour,, such as holding a paw in the air, maintaining the sleepy head to the floor, holding a paw over the face.

Usually these are taught as self ending behaviours. ie the dog hears the cue, performs the behaviour, we click and the dog stops the behaviour and takes the reward.

I have always found the process of "delaying the click for longer" begins to punish the behaviour. Perhaps this is my fault, perhaps I didn't graduate the delay quite finely enough.

Certainly my emphasis on training is attaching the cue to a behaviour and having a good quality behaviour of good strength. As soon as I see the response from the dog or a quick response (excellent memory skills) and a high quality I want to get in there with the click. This "no-click" area gives us more trouble than the "when to click" problem ever did!

From this history of teaching you can see my dogs expect their click fairly promptly, and the delaying click will shoot them off to other behaviours. To teach simple sustained behaviours I use the quick click on achievement and then deliver the food to the dog in the sustained behaviour. This is a great technique for the sit stay, down stay etc, where the food can be eaten in situ.

But for behaviours that the dog would have to finish to be able to be rewarded, such as paw over face (tired) or a walking high five, I use the self running sequence technique and repeat the behaviour three times in a row.

SEQUENCE OF SAME BEHAVIOUR

STEP 1

"tired"   "tired"   "tired"   cues
   tired → tired → tired   behaviours

STEP 2

"tired"   "tired"   cues
   tired → tired → tired   behaviours

STEP 3

"tired"   cues
   tired → tired → tired   behaviours

When using the sequence technique for the same behaviour I don't use the click, I use the food delivery as the end of the behaviour. Mind you, if Mabel is doing an exceptionally good "tired", paw over face, then she can't see me deliver the food (since her paw is covering her eyes) and I use the click to get her out of the behaviour!

BALANCING THE SEQUENCE

Very often we put together a self running sequence that contains behaviours of different value to the dog. For a dog keen on retrieve the "wait" part is going to be hard to keep the quality, the fast dog will find the pick-up hard to control their speed.

For a clumsy dog finding a contact point will be difficult, particularly if the clumsy dog is focused on the next obstacle prior to leaving the contact obstacle.

For the steady dog, animated heeling is going to difficult to "pump up" for.

Very often the sequence contains a mixture of behaviours, some of which the dog prefers over other behaviours. If you keep practising the behaviours in the sequence, the stronger behaviours will tear apart the weaker ones.

For the fast retrieve dog, the pick up will start to fall apart - with travel on after pick-up or a fumbling collection. You must be very alert to the chaining of the behaviours causing damage to individual behaviours. You know through teaching each of these behaviours and keeping data on the quantity of batches each behaviour has taken to get to the sequence pre-entry test how long, and how hard, the dog has had to work to achieve quality, fluency and reliability.

These behaviours will continue to need extra training.

sequences are rarely of equal behaviours

some behaviours will weaken and some
strengthen in practising a sequence

the practice sessions of the individual behaviours
need to maintain the balance

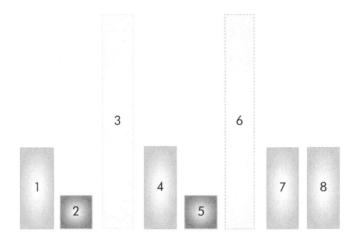

behaviours 3 & 6 get more training in relation
to behaviours 2 & 5.

POINT OF REWARD

When practising sequences or groups of behaviours remember that
the behaviour directly preceding the delivery of the reward will get
more reinforcement than the other behaviours. This can cause the
other behaviours to deteriorate as the dog tries to get to the
rewarding behaviour as quickly as possible.

This is a great strategy used to advantage in retrieve. If the reward
point is always on "give" then the dog will hurry the other behaviours
to get to that point, but if the dog finds the capture of the article or
toy the point of reward, and more rewarding than your food delivery,
the behaviours will be fast up to the pick up, and noticeable slower
after that point. If this is the case, close up the give point to the pick
up point so that the self reinforcing aspect of the pick up (capture) is
associated with the give (release).

If you are teaching the dog to beg or rollover, the first part of the
behaviours, sit and down, can deteriorate when the second and third
parts are getting the click and food delivery.

You can re-balance this with a click for the first behaviour and a
quick cue for the second behaviour which gets the food delivery. It

would do no harm by this stage to click both, but make sure you come in promptly with the cue for the second behaviour straight on the tail of the first behaviour's click.

Ideally you balance the training by only a couple of sequences then a click and reward for the first behaviour alone:

click and reward

We can't fault dogs for being smart, so if you need one behaviour in place to be able to teach a second behaviour, do not punish the dog for anticipating and remember you may need the opening behaviour for future occasions, NOT attached to a "beg" or anything else!

MERGING CUES

If you are grouping behaviours together that happen simultaneously it is easier if the cues can all be given simultaneously.

An excellent example of merging behaviours is the dog responding to the cue in a new location.

If we teach the behaviours in front of us or to our side, the dog will become conditioned that this location is where the behaviour will occur. The location is a separate behaviour.

When the dog is at 10 feet and the sit is cued, the dog runs a short self running sequence of moving the the location and then going into the sit.

To teach the dog "out there" is a great place to be and just another behaviour you can play a wonderful game of "stay there whilst I throw the reward to you".

Choose a suitable training floor where the dog can see and easily collect the food from the floor.

Begin with throwing a piece of food to 10 feet, let the dog run out and collect.

As soon as the dog looks up at you click, and toss out another piece of food. Even if the dog has travelled back half the distance, throw the food over their head out to 10 feet.

I use an exaggerated over arm throw, where my hand is above my head. I have this hand loaded with food and ready to throw before the dog looks up from eating. They will start to see this gesture out of the corner of their eye and eat and stay there waiting for the next throw (I told you dogs were smart).

The hand signal initially stimulates the behaviour of waiting out there.

Once the dog is responding to this hand gesture and no longer travels in, add a verbal cue "out", and then give the hand gesture.

Train this in many places, build the strength, and then add the "out there" behaviour with the sit or down or whatever you want at the distance.

You can mix and match the simultaneous cues with a hand gesture for "out there" mixed with the verbal cue "sit", or the other way around.

If the reward continues to go out to the dog, you will reinforce the success and build the dog's confidence that being at a distance is just as rewarding a location as being near by.

I teach formal heelwork as two separate behaviors:

1. Find the heel location.
   This is taught whilst I am still, the dog can move to the correct
   location from any direction.

2. Trot.
   The dog must be able to trot on cue, I teach this with a target
   stick, and progress the trotting action until the dog can
   perform a collected trot. This is not taught in the heel position.

Each of these behaviours has a cue:

1. Find the heel location.   cue = hand signal

2. Trot.   cue = verbal "ticking" sound

The two behaviours will not be merged together until both behaviours
are performing with good strength on a single cue. The trotting action
will be moved from the target stick target to an outstretched hand.

As the dog is started on the trotting action at arm's length the hand
will move to the heel cue and the two behaviours can come together.
I can continuously give both cues, the heel hand signal and the
trotting verbal cue for the first few steps of the merged behaviour.

I will make sure that the dog learns to merge with either behaviour
first to give flexibility:

STEP 1

Dog is cued "trot" trotting on outstretched arm

Arm moves to heel hand signal

heelwork

STEP 2

Arm starts in heel hand signal dog arrives

Dog is cued to trot on verbal cue

heelwork

By building this flexibility in at this stage the dog will be able to offer either behaviour when the other is in place. If the dog is trotting but loses position after a turn, it will be able to move into location, and the opposite, if the dog is in location after a turn it will be able to initiate "trot".

If they are always cued into the merge in the same order, ie location first and then trot, the dog will only be able to initiate them in that cued order and not "repair" a situation that has slipped.

This would be the same with retrieve over a jump, neither behaviour would become habituated to being first.

But in some cases we want one behaviour first, perhaps the sit before a beg, or the lay down before a rollover. So as the merged part of beg is cued, the sit will always come first. (The action of lifting into a beg is the same whether the dog starts from a sit position or a standing position, if starting from the sit it is the beg, if starting from the stand it is the "high" walking). We certainly do not want the dog initiating the rollover from standing, as the impact of the dog's shoulder to the floor could cause injury.

BEG

Dog is sitting "sit"

Dog cued to "up"

sit beg

HIGH WALK

Dog is sitting "standing"

Dog cued to "up"

high walk

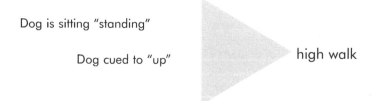

ROLLOVER

Dog is cued to "down"

Dog cued to "rollover"   rollover

... BUT NOT THIS

Dog is standing

Dog cued to "rollover"   rollover

The final cue for merged behaviour can be either of the component cues, provided you do not want either behaviour merged at a later point with a new behaviour. It this case you need to consider a new cue for the merged behaviour.

I see bright dogs work out the components themselves, and adjust their sitting position, for instance, depending on the location. But it heavily depends on the dog making this deduction: "Ah . . . the other sit".

I keep the cues separate to be able to attach the heel position cue, and merge it with walking backwards and sideways, and perhaps in a high-walk. I will use trotting in recall, and in circles around me, not always in the heel position. I would not employ either cue in the merged context to allow the option of separating that behaviour to be called on in another group.

SEPARATING OUT THE CUES

Very often we have taught a behaviour as a merge of other behaviours and we need to be able to separate them into individual behaviours.

An obvious simple behaviour is the dog sitting in front of you.

You want the sit to be called upon separately from being in front of you, and quite likely you have brought into this merge some direct eye contact, the dog is watching you.

For a formal retrieve I need the dog to be able to sit by my side (not only in front), and look forward (not at me).

To be able to successfully label the individual behaviours or locations look for commonality with other merges. Such as standing in front, laying down in front. Cue the dog to come "in front" on verbal cue, and use the signal to indicate the sit, or a down or a stand still.

By keeping one behaviour on visual cue and the other behaviour on verbal, we can switch around either combinations, until the dogs goes: "Aha, got it!"

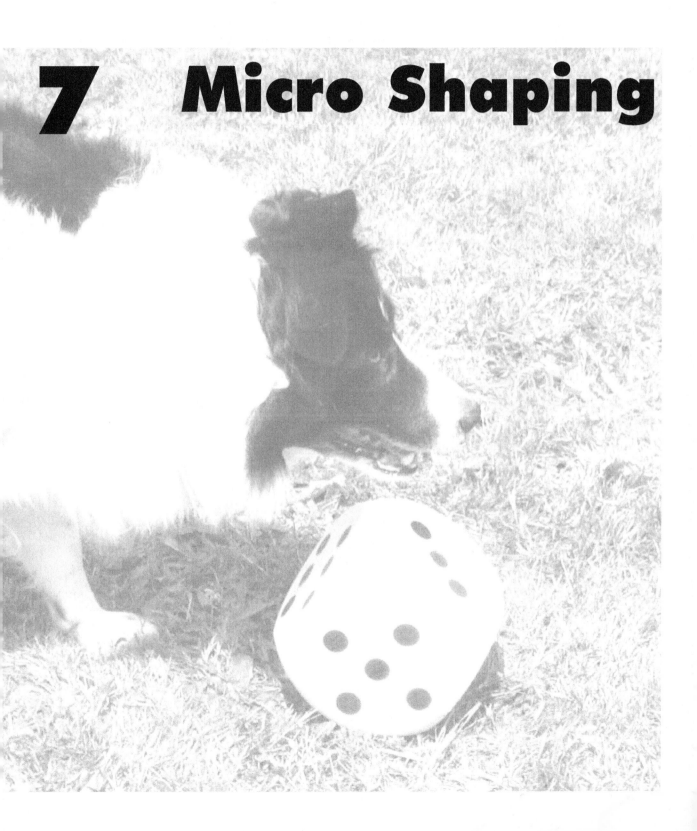

7 Micro Shaping

As your confidence in clicker training grows you will become more comfortable with shaping and find it increasingly fascinating. There are certain behaviours that cannot be acquired or isolated by any other means and there is a joy in watching the dog learn and explore our goals.

That shaping tail wag is unique to shaping and carries a great degree of humour. We know the dogs are enjoying themselves and the process becomes reinforcing for us at the same time.

If you have a clear picture of a behaviour you want to teach, often the difficult questions is whether to lure or whether to shape. The choice of method is affected by:

▶ the limitations dictated by your skills

   - your ability to anticipate what and when to click
   - your ability to observe and see the finer parts of the behaviour
   - the placement of the food to set up the dog for easy success

▶ how much choice should the learner have in the process

   - choice gives greater room for the dog to learn from error
   - too much choice can leave the dog adrift

▶ whether the end result requires a high degrees of accuracy

   - the dog may learn poor movements without physical luring or help

▶ what type of cue will trigger the end behaviour

   - the lure or target cue is very strongly associated through the first attachment during learning

▶ whether the final behaviour will be on direct cue or indirect cue

   - if the dog needs to complete the behaviour from an environment of object cue, or from a previous behaviour in a chain, the new cue can be hard to attach from directed learning

In reality all learning is a mixture of luring, targeting, barrier training and free shaping.

At each extreme:

    luring is directed learning

       and

    free shaping is self-directed learning

It has been found in studies from the education system that the acquisition of learning by self-directed teaching will have greater impact and longer memory.

Ideally all errors should be in the self-directed area then we should never make mistakes again. Hah!

In the dog's learning world they self teach that biting a wasp may hurt and jumping in the pond requires you to shut your mouth. These lessons can only be learned from the experience, or the error, and fortunately for us dogs are exceptionally good at this form of learning. They have good memory skills and abilities to puzzle solve on the job. (But that doesn't stop my 12 year old Kiwi still biting wasps.)

Learning is a path filled with choices. We set up situations where the quantity of choice available is at our discretion, depending on how much error you want the dog to experience. With clicker training we should not be afraid of error being an important part of their learning. The errors are only ever "punished" with the no-click, the dog makes the choice whether they wish to pursue that area or mistakes again or not. We simply do not pay.

If the learning is heavily directed, with little or no degree of choice, the dog becomes learning dependent. They have poor ability to make choices and often wait to be told what to do. This is sometimes the end result of coercive teaching, even if the coercion is without punishment it will still have the effect of limiting the dog's cognitive abilities.

If the learning is at the other extreme with no direction, the dog can acquire very bad habits that will be hard to change. First learning is usually the strongest learning and this is the experience that will have the greatest impact.

I remember a local farmer telling me about teaching his sheepdog pups to keep out of the way of vehicles around the farm. The dogs are loose all the time and need an understanding of wheels. He would take the youngsters, from around 6 weeks, and let them play around when he was mucking out, or moving stuff with the wheel

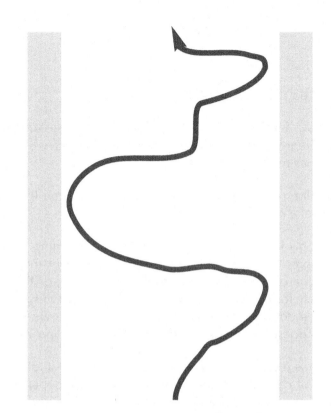

heavily directed
little degree of choice, forced to
learn a very exact way

non-directed
with little guidance and high
degree of error

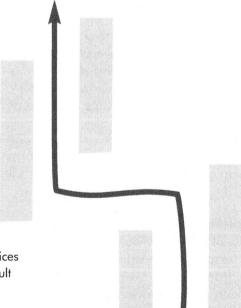

the middle choice, some
guidance, but room for choices
and flexibility in the end result

The behaviour is part directed
and part self-directed.

directed learning:
    barrier shaping,
    targeting or luring

non directed learning:
    free shaping

directed learning:
    barrier shaping,
    targeting or luring

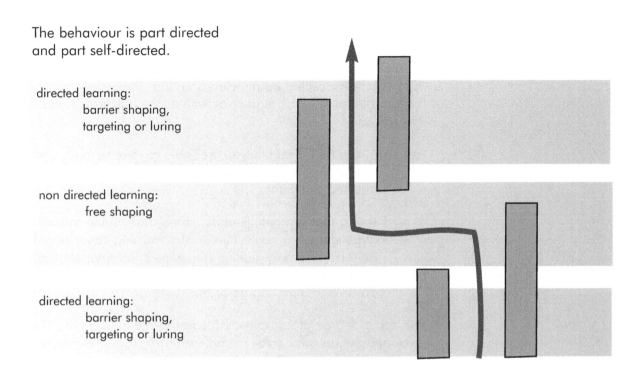

barrow. Very quickly the pups learned to keep away from the wheels. These were "safe" wheels.

If, at the other extreme, the pups had not been exposed to "safe" wheels they would have to learn from the dangerous experience of motorised vehicles, cars and tractors, harvesters and other lethal machines. But equally it would have been a difficult skills to teach a dog if taught with direct learning, ie cued to move back every time. They would become dependent on that cue for a long time, perhaps for life.

At the same time he played these games with the pups he also made a choice which to keep, an ability to keep clear of wheels was a major "keeping" factor on this busy farm.

SOME DEGREE OF DIRECTION
CAN FORM GOOD HABITS

TOO MUCH CAN REMOVE A DOG'S
FLEXIBILITY IN THE END BEHAVIOUR.

In breaking down the behaviours we can spot that certain elements are more suited to direct luring and certain to free shaping.

Our choice for setting up directed and non-directed learning will have an impact on the learner as well as the outcome of the behaviour.

> A dog that is mentally active, able to to remember, make decisions, is physically self aware and will thrive in non-directed situations.

> A dog that is mentally under stress, habituated to learning dependency, or has a diminished learning capacity will perform poorly in making decisions and remembering from the learning. For them free shaping can cause them to shut down or a high degree of frustration.

But some degree of non-directed learning will develop this dog, provided the area for error is small and only increases as the dog's learning skills increases.

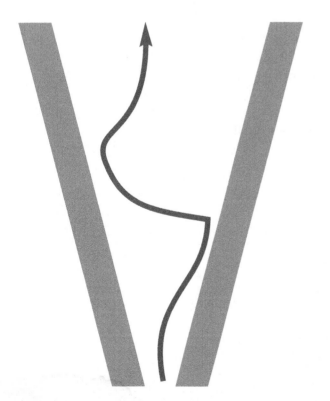

Building a dog's cognitive capacity and learning skills by increasing the degree of choices they make.

The mentally active dog can also thrive on luring, since their learning skills will be tuned in to what they are doing as they are directed. But too much directed learning can frustrate them and cause more problems.

Lessons can be set to be dog orientated or behaviour orientated:

> Are you developing the dog's learning skills and choose behaviours and teaching strategies to enhance that?

> > or

> Are you focused on the end behaviour only?

Ideally we build a dog who becomes a good, first class learner to whom we can teach any behaviour we choose.

BALANCING THE BUILDING

The balance can be achieved through breaking down the behaviours and finding which behaviours would be ideally learned with directed teaching and those under non-directed teaching.

Remember that an excessive amount of one or the other can lead to more problems.

The small parts of the behaviour need to be examined for:

1. Would a degree of error in learning enhance the dog's awareness?

2. Will the dog struggle to acquire the skill without direction?

3. Can the lure or barrier be faded without losing the behaviour?

4. Can we ensure the first experience is beneficial?

STEP 1

► Make a list of the behaviours you will teach.
  These will be taught individually and not sequenced until strength is acquired in each. Do not teach as part of the chain, teach as individuals.

> ▶ Select which behaviours MUST be either directed or non-directed

> ▶ Let the other behaviours balance the learning to benefit the dog

TURNING A CIRCLE

Not just one behaviour but at least three MOVEMENTS.

By breaking down this behaviour into the individual movements (which is what the dog learns and the click attaches itself to) we can see where to lure and where to free shape.

Turning in a circle	Directed	Non-Directed
Turning away	✔	
Degree of turn	✔	
Coming back to face me		✔

I choose the turning away as a directed movement since it is contrary to nearly everything I have teach the dog, which is to focus on me. In addition if I am holding the reward, turning away would be a very difficult movement to free shape.

I choose the degree of turn to be directed since this exercise needs to be performed with speed, but not silly speed, and I use it to increase the flexibility of the dog's spine. Some dogs when turning around keep a straight spine and rotate around their shoulder, others will bend their backs.

I choose the coming back to face me as free shaping, since this is the part I want the dog to understand where they have to finish the behaviour. I want some degree of error in this learning to ensure that as the dog goes through the first two parts of the behaviour I have mental focus on the end part. This is also the element that will get the highest reinforcement when the three behaviours are sequenced.

In practice I use a target stick for the first two behaviours and free shaping for the last part.

MICRO SHAPING

This technique has been developed to ensure the highest possible results of accuracy and understanding from the free shaping process. The power of free shaping is unquestionable in the effect it has developing the learner, but if there is a disadvantage it can be the de-motivating lack of success and the possibility of inaccurate learning.

Very often when a dog is shaping the rate of reinforcement can be as low as 30%. This will depress the dog's desire to progress which limits the length of time the dog will continue to shape, and how many criteria they can acquire in one lesson.

A typical free shaping session often consists of waiting for the dog to find the behaviour we are looking for. In between their fruitless attempts are not only the previously learned behaviours, sit, wave a paw, bow, spin, walk back, sneeze, shake, but many other secondary behaviours of looking away, nodding a head, fidgeting, licking the lips.

In a session to shape a dog to stand on a low stool a dog can interact with the stool in several different ways, a look, a paw, a nose, a go round, a lay down in addition to the usual doggy behaviours of "I'm thinking ... hang on a minute".

We have recorded the data for these type of shaping sessions on 28 different dogs and trainers shaping for this behaviour over a maximum of ten minutes.

The dogs came from mixed learning histories. All had been clicker training for at least six months and all had experience of free shaping.

The trainers came from a variety of different training backgrounds. Some had only a small amount of experience free shaping and some were considerably more experienced.

The definition of free shaping here is the trainer not participating in the learning in any way, except by the clicker and the placement of the food. They were all sitting in a chair and not allowed to speak or cue.

Firstly we were looking for the rate of reinforcement (number of clicks) per minute, against the number of behaviours offered.

REINFORCEMENT RATE FOR FREE SHAPING "STAND ON STOOL".

Time of one minute	1	2	3	4	5	6	7	8	9	10
Sample (Dog No 7)										
no of behaviours offered	18	18	19	26	5	6	6	11	3	6
no of clicks per minute	3	7	3	2	0	3	2	4	1	0
rate of success	17%	39%	16%	8%	0%	50%	33%	36%	33%	0%
	average=25%									
Average all dogs										
no of behaviours offered	22	19	20	13	8	12	22	6	12	6
no of clicks per minute	18	12	5	6	2	8	5	3	2	3
rate of success	82%	63%	20%	46%	25%	67%	22%	50%	17%	50%
	average = 44%									

Some trainers opened up well with a high rate of reinforcement looking for generalised interaction with the stool. But after 10 minutes most dogs had started to give up, some acquired the behaviour but only had a fragile hold on the behaviour as could be seen by the rate of reinforcement NOT increasing. Other behaviours were still being offered between the successful ones.

I wouldn't like to learn with that rate of success.

I want the dog to have a high rate of reinforcement, somewhere averaging 90%. This is my key criterion. For a dog with that degree of reinforcement they continue to shape for much longer and increase criteria much more soundly.

By placing my priority on the rate of reinforcement staying high, I must achieve this by breaking the behaviour down into small, limited movements that the dog can repeat easily and develop the muscle and memory for.

> By "micro-shaping" the dog can develop a sound opening behaviour in connection with the object.

> By "micro-shaping" the dog can be taught with a high degree of accuracy but still make the choices that free shaping benefits the learner.

> By "micro-shaping" the behaviour becomes strong from the outset.

By "micro-shaping" the dog develops mental strength and high levels of motivation from the clarity of the communication without the restraints of directed learning.

I like micro-shaping!

These are the results from 7 dogs learning the stand on stool

MICRO SHAPING "STAND ON STOOL".

Time of one minute	1	2	3	4	5	6	7	8	9	10
Average all dogs										
no of behaviours offered	22	26	25	26	24	24	22	23	25	26
no of clicks per minute	21	24	24	26	23	22	20	20	24	26
rate of success	95%	92%	96%	100%	96%	92%	91%	87%	96%	100%
	average =		95%							

This is the sort of learning I want!

Did the dogs all stand on the stool by the end ? No.

But the dogs that had been micro shaped were still offering lots of repetitions of the desired criteria at the end of the session and went on to complete the whole behaviour within the next five minutes training.

I have not had the opportunity to measure enough dogs trained in many different behaviours either way to compare sufficient results. (I'm talking 100 dogs each way on 30 different behaviours to get effective results).

But I like the results the micro-shaping is giving us:

▶ happy dogs

▶ dogs keen to keep on trying for at least 10 minutes without tiring

▶ behaviours that are very, very strong

▶ behaviours that need less reinforcement training after the behaviour is acquired

▶ behaviours that are generalising quickly

▶ trainers that are much clearer what to do and how to do it

(Phew, less training time!)

THE PLAN FOR MICRO SHAPING

This technique will need a small amount of planning and practice to acquire.

Prepare your food, make sure it will be easily and quickly eaten, this is going to be very fast work. Not the day for crumbly food, or food you need to break up before you deliver.

Find a timer to set at one minute that will audibly tell you the end of the minute.

Choose a behaviour that opens with a very specific movement that you can easily identify, such as:

▶ side stepping
  begins with the paw lifting to move sideways, followed by back paw matching front paw, followed by the other front and back paw closing in

▶ paws onto object, stool, brick or plate
  begins with taking note of the object, then approach to object, standing within range to touch with a paw, paw lifts to tap, paw lifts to press, weight changes, other paw touches, weight balanced on both paws

▶ picking up article
  dog looks at article, dog steps towards article, dog makes face contact with article, dog pushes into article, dog opens mouth at article, mouth closes around article, article moves, article leaves floor, dog takes step carrying article

Some of these behaviour will take several sessions. It is irrelevant how long it takes but that the dog is comfortable and strong in each criteria before moving on and the final result is of high quality, strong with flexibility in application.

Take a seat so that you can delivery quickly to the dog or floor without excessive body language.

Prepare at least 25 pieces of food ready to delivery without any delay.

Set up the situation so that the dog clearly understands this is a free shaping session. The dogs will usually anticipate this when you begin to count out food and then take a seat.

Have a clear picture of the opening movement. Let's look at the stepping onto stool.

The opening movement will be a look at the object. Click for the look and feed the dog so that the only part of their body that needs to move to collect the food is their head. Use either your hand or place the food to the floor. Repeat this feed - look - click - feed, cycle for at least the first minute.

By feeding in a very specific location and so quickly that the dog cannot leave the spot when they hear the click, we are limiting the movement that the dog will need to do to be successful again. I expect this movement to be rewarded at least 20 times in a minute, that is every 3 seconds. You will need to be fast.

The next step is to introduce flexibility or generalise this stage or criteria. As you begin the next minute make sure the dog is looking at the stool from a slightly different position. Over the next three minutes, increase the distance the dog relocates around the object. Try to go for different angles to begin with rather than increase the distance. The hardest criteria would be the dog turning away from you to look at the stool. Leave that location until last.

The next step is go back to an easy location and to let the dog look and take one step to the stool. If the dog is by the stool place the food so that the dog makes the movement to place itself ready for the paw to lift and tap the stool.

Remember between every minute take a short break of at least half a minute. Pick up the stool so the dog cannot keep shaping, this removes the cue for the duration of the break. Restock with food and begin again each time at exactly the point you left off. If necessary lure the dog to the exact location.

Do not exceed 10 one minute sessions. Enough food! The dog will be urging you to go on, but leave the next sessions for another day.

Sit back for a moment and visualise the final behaviour. The dog is standing looking at you and you give the cue "stool".

What is the first thing they must do?

Look for it. Sometimes it will be to the front of them or it may even be behind them. As soon as they have seen the stool what is the next thing they will do?

Move towards it. Next they must arrive, or plan to arrive so that they can step fluently onto the stool. They must have the flexibility to arrive from different directions, build it into the learning.

If they arrive too close they can knock the stool, if they arrive too fast they may push the stool with the momentum of getting onto it.

By shaping each step really solidly and with built in flexibility, we can as near as possible guarantee this is how the dog will perform the behaviour. If at any time something untoward happens, the dog approaches from a bad angle, or slips when getting onto the stool, they will be able to revert to the solid step that was acquired prior to that error.

There is one element that I hope you will all see from this process is the smiling faces on the dogs! Phew, they're up to speed at last!

To review step by step what you will do:

MICRO SHAPING
STEP 1 - PREPARATION

- ▶ choose a behaviour that you have planned the possible progress for. Make a "progress map". (see Appendix C)

- ▶ make sure you can observe the progress in small movements. Setting a small dog on a table and sitting at the table makes the observation of leg movements easier to see.

- ▶ think where the food placement will be to restrict the movement

- ▶ prepare food that is fast to deliver and fast to eat

STEP 2 - OPEN THE LESSON

▶ take up 25 pieces of food

▶ place the object to the floor and take a seat

▶ set the timer to one minute and start it

▶ if necessary lure the dog to the opening point

STEP 3 - FAST AND CONSISTENT

▶ deliver the food in the same location every time, to mouth or floor

▶ allow at least 20 repetitions of the same behaviour

▶ plan to move to the next criteria when you see 5 consecutive fluent strong repetitions

STEP 4 - WORK IN ONE MINUTE SESSIONS

▶ only work for approximately 60 seconds. This is very intense concentration and motor skills (from you of course). The muscles the dog is using will get tired as well.

▶ do not exceed more than 10 sessions in one lesson

▶ make a note of which point you finished at

STEP 5 - BUILD IN FLEXIBILITY

▶ for each movement that you will fix, broaden the dog's experience by including one minute sessions with variation in each session

▶ increase distance only within the limitations of your food placement

STEP 6 - DON'T RUSH

▶ by taking each stage with care and precision you will dramatically reduce your post teaching practice

▶ the object, the stool, is the cue at this time

> ▶ only micro shape one behaviour at a time

> ▶ add the final cue when the whole behaviour is completed, fluent, strong and with variety

STEP 7 - KEEP RECORDS

To calculate the success rate you will need a pen and paper, calculator, and small dish. This is the "wrong dish".

1. Count 25 pieces of food into your hand. Most dogs can offer up to 25 successful behaviours in one minute

2. For every behaviour that is offered and NOT successful place a piece of food in this dish. Make sure the dog cannot see this movement otherwise it could become a punisher.

3. At the end of the session count:

the total you took into your hand	= 25	(A)
the pieces of food still in your hand	= 3	(B)
subtract B from A	= 22	(C)

    The dog offered 22 behaviours.
    This is the rate of behaviours per minute

the pieces of food in the wrong dish	= 2	(D)
subtract D from C	= 20	(E)

    The dog offered 20 successful behaviours.
    This is the number of clicks per minute, rate of success

    divide E, by C and multiply by 100   = % success rate.

    $$^{20}/_{22} \times 100 \quad = 91\%$$

(Micro-shaping record sheets are in Appendix A)

STEP 8 - ANALYSING PROGRESS

Look for patterns emerging. Very often it is not the particular behaviour that we should closely examine, but the overall progress rate of the dog's ability to learn.

1. Does the rate of success increase, decrease or stay the same through one session?

2. Does the rate of success vary between different type of behaviours? How will you classify types of behaviours?

3. If the rate of success is varying could that particular criteria be too large a step for the dog to achieve the success rate? Does it need to be broken into smaller movements to keep up the success rate?

4. Does the dog tire sooner or later as they build their experience in shaping?

5. When increasing flexibility by adding variation to a stage does the dog acquire a higher success rate sooner? Does this mean the dog is able to generalise the behaviour much quicker?

It would be useful to be able to measure the comparative strength of a micro-shaped behaviour in every day use, compared to a lured behaviour or a traditionally shaped behaviour. But the dog's experience will affect the results and it is difficult to find two comparative behaviours to be able to teach. This becomes the area of the trainer's ability to observe and feel the strength and response of the dog.

SHAPING FOR WICKED FUN

Shaping does not need to be with a purpose. We can use the very exacting micro shaping strategy for specific teaching, but the dogs also enjoy the shaping game itself.

I still play the "nothing twice" game to keep a dog alert. Particularly useful for the older dogs that are not under strict training regimes. I will place several objects on the floor, mostly toys and play objects and click for anything the dog does, provided they have not done this before.

The environment for this session needs to be very specific and dissimilar to any other training session. The dog will learn to offer one behaviour, and then dismiss it and move onto something new. This could be a major hazard for a dog in micro-shaping, where they repeat and repeat the same behaviour.

Avoid confusing the dogs, the game is not worth a confused dog.

Dance the dance is another game I play. I only use a large, specific mat for this. The dog will get clicked for any movement on the mat that resembles "dancing". They can jig, fidget, goon around, flirt. I started this for the freestyle training to see what the dogs would offer rather than just stick to my limited perceptions of what I could teach. Mabel designed a diagonal jump backwards like a spring lamb, and she also has the "Tart's Swank", which is a sashay of the shoulders with a large paw wave.

Shaping is tremendous fun, and having no specific agenda is a quality experience for both participants. Our classes enjoy these sessions with only one dog entertaining us at a time, and they constantly surprise us with what they can do with objects that we never though of!

Appendix A

**CLICKER TRAINERS
COMPETENCY ASSESSMENT PROGRAM (CAP)**

**FOUNDATION   - LEVEL 1
NOVICE   - LEVEL 2
INTERMEDIATE - LEVEL 3**

COMPETENCY ASSESSMENT PROGRAM (CAP)

Clicker Training is a fast growing teaching method that has evolved into thousands of different classes and interests. Essentially the definition of a "clicker trainer" is a person who trains using a clicker. Competency is not directly measurable by the description, some clicker trainers are reaching for the sky and able to achieve astonishing results, some clicker trainers are simply adding the clicker to an existing program of training, which may or may not be coercive.

I believe the true power of clicker training is seeded in allowing the dog to self teach and in particular through the method of capturing the behaviour. The canine ownership of the learning results in very secure cue association and reliability of quality. The dog truly becomes involved in the learning process, becomes highly motivated and teaches us poor humans a thing or two about learning!

To gain access to this powerful method the teacher needs to be skilled, very self aware, observant, able to analyse, able to adjust the teaching to suit that particular dog at that particular time. As they develop their skills their understanding of the process deepens and they are able to transfer the learning to other animals and other fields of interest. They have genuinely learned to communicate with another species through skilled use of the clicker.

The Competency Assessment Program (CAP) is designed to serve two purposes:

▶ to provide a clear pathway, with marked steps for learners to gain their skill, knowledge and understanding

▶ to provide a certification system validating the competency of clicker trainers

The assessment system is not intended to highlight what a person has not achieved, but what a person has accomplished and give confidence at their achieved level.

All elements must attain a pass. Assessment is given at three grades:

1   Pass. Demonstrates some skill, knowledge and understanding, but many areas in need of further development

2   Merit. Demonstrates good skill, knowledge and understanding, some areas in need of further development

3   Distinction. Demonstrates excellent skill, knowledge and understanding, in need of little or no further development

Achievement in the lower level with Merit or above is required to progress. Assessors need Distinction in the higher class to assess, ie Distinction in Level 2 to assess Level 1.

Assessment for each level takes approximately 15-20 minutes. The assessor will be looking at the process of clicker training through the trainer's technique, ability to be flexible and meet the needs of the dog and develop positive learning experience for the dog and communicate effectively.

At no time will the dog be under test

The trainer will be expected to pre-select the exercises to suit the dog and the situation of the test.

FOUNDATION LEVEL 1

This level is assessing the basic handling skills of the rewards, clicker, lure and target stick/hand together with the trainer's ability to communicate with the dog without coercion, their observation and decision making skills. Trainers would be expected to be able to add cues, names and signals to behaviours and have shaped and lured simple behaviours.

NOVICE LEVEL 2

This level is assessing the trainer's ability to secure a solid foundation in achieving a consistent quality and reliability to cue. So often trainers are so captured by the brilliance and creativity of dogs that they forge ahead shaping complex behaviours without the knowledge and skills to make the behaviours reliable in quality and reliable to their cue. Anywhere, anytime, any place. This teacher skill is essential to obtain the full value and strength of clicker training.

Shaping skills with high frequency reward rate will be observed, the ability to communicate unsuccessful behaviours, fade the lure and target stick, develop the dog's physical fluency through repetitive exercises and build variable duration of a behaviour.

Achieving Foundation and Novice level is quite sufficient for most dog owners. They will be able to train the basic behaviours required of society, with reliability in a range of situations. Those wishing to enter sports, train dogs for work or develop behaviour modification programs should follow the curriculum and be assessed at Intermediate and Advanced Levels.

INTERMEDIATE LEVEL 3

The assessor will be looking for a broad range of captured behaviours and complex exercises derived from chaining, merging and sequencing. Precision shaping skills will be observed with multiple targeting. Trainers will need to demonstrate their skills of affecting the behaviour through varying the timing of the click, using different reward ratios and rewards. Evidence of data collection and analysis will be reviewed.

ADVANCED LEVEL 4

Trainers may be assessed in the field of behaviour modification or high level performance and working dogs.

Trainers at this level will need to be able to make significant behavioural changes
through the use of the clicker, with case history or video evidence. Trainers will need to
be able to plan to develop specific learning programs in dogs with learning difficulties
and be familiar with teaching emotional control, extinguishing and replacing behaviours.

> OR

Trainers should be able to demonstrate a high quality performance or demonstration
with durability. Trainers will need to be able to plan to develop a specific learning
program for dogs in advanced performance work or working dogs.

TAKING THE TEST

Assessment days are be held through the year as advertised in Teaching Dogs Magazine
or on the website. These may be in conjunction with other events or workshops, and at
approved testing centres. The cost per test will be in the region of £7-£10 ($12-18)
depending on the cost of the venue.

Clubs, classes and events will be able to host the CAPs and trainers are able to take the
test by video. Assessors for all levels will be required to shadow assess to qualify.

Trainers may take any assessment as many times as they wish until a Distinction is
achieved. Trainers may review with the assessor their grades and discuss areas in need
of improvement. Details of assessment opportunities are published regularly in Teaching
Dogs Magazine and on the website: www.learningaboutdogs.com

FOUNDATION LEVEL 1 TEST

The test will be taken in a small area and behaviours chosen by the trainer appropriate
to that area. The dog may be clicked and rewarded for each behaviour. The assessors
will give the trainer a choice of behaviours to shape.

AT NO TIME WILL THE DOG BE UNDER TEST

1. Demonstrate 6 repetitions of the same behaviour
2. Demonstrate 6 repetitions of another behaviour with only a verbal cue
3. Demonstrate 6 repetition of a third behaviour of a variable duration. The length of the
    behaviour must be appropriate to the skills of the dog.

4. Demonstrate a developing behaviour 6 times with a target stick or target hand

5. Free shape a new behaviour without luring or cue

The assessor will look for the trainer demonstrating that they:

1. Handle food rewards safely and efficiently.

2. Deliver food rewards from hand or pocket.

3. Deliver from a reserve kept off the handler.

4. Operate the clicker in either hand with a non-visual movement.

5. Hold the target stick/hand, clicker and rewards and deliver food effectively.

6. Give reasons for their choice of reward.

7. Attached a verbal cue to a behaviour

8. Give a cue without excessive body language or unnecessary repetition.

9. Have taught the dog to respond to the cue without excessive hesitation.

10. Give the click appropriately to effectively communicate the rewarded behaviour.

11. Deliver the reward with fluency and good timing to encourage further learning.

12. Use a target stick or hand on a behaviour that is still under development showing that the dog is focused on the target and the dog responds promptly to the target cue.

NOVICE LEVEL 2 TEST

The test will be taken in a small area and behaviours chosen by the trainer appropriate to that area. The dog may be clicked and rewarded for each behaviour. The assessor will give the trainer a choice of behaviours to shape. The assessor will be looking for a consistently high quality of the behaviour through each repetition.

At no time will the dog be under test

1. Demonstrate 10 repetitions of the same behaviour to a single cue where the behaviour was captured through targeting and the target has been faded. The trainer must demonstrate the history of the learning.

2. Demonstrate 10 repetitions of another behaviour to a single cue

3. Demonstrate 10 repetitions of a behaviour of variable duration

    Of these three behaviours one must be to a verbal cue only, and one must be to a signal cue only. During these 30 repetitions the trainer will be asked to change their location relative to the dog, change the location of the dog, change the location or type of reward. At some time a distraction will be introduced. The trainer will also demonstrate the behaviour is not present unless cued.

4. Temporarily change the cue for one of the behaviours already demonstrated.

5. Free shape a new behaviour that is a stand alone physical movement

6.   Free shape a new behaviour that is interaction with an object

The assessor will look for the trainer demonstrating that they:

1.   Have taught a behaviour through targeting where the target is no longer the cue.
2.   Have transferred a targeted behaviour to a new target or cue.
3.   Have achieved and maintained fluency in 3 different behaviours of high quality.
4.   Discriminatively click/not click behaviour to a pre determined quality.
5.   Maintain the quality through distractions.
6.   Can change the cue attached to a behaviour.
7.   Have attached a reliable verbal cue and non-verbal cue to a behaviour
8.   Can shape a new behaviour that is a physical movement without luring or targeting and a new behaviour that is interaction with an object without luring or targeting

INTERMEDIATE LEVEL 3 TEST

The test will be taken in a small area and behaviours chosen by the trainer appropriate to that area.

The trainer is expected to be able to collect a series of behaviours together that are individually of finished quality. When the behaviours are collected the trainer will not be expected to reward or reinforce the individual behaviours except at the end of each repetition.

AT NO TIME WILL THE DOG BE UNDER TEST

1.   Demonstrate 5 repetitions of a chain of at least 5different behaviours. The chain to be commenced with a single cue.
2.   Demonstrate 5 repetitions of the same sequence of 5 different behaviours, each of which must have a single cue.
3.   Demonstrate 5 repetitions of a behaviour that is a merge of at least 3 separate behaviours. The trainer will need to demonstrate each of the separate behaviours first.
4.   Demonstrate they can put together a new complex behaviour from the individual behaviours already demonstrated as agreed with the assessor.
5.   Free shape a complex behaviour.
6.   Present data collected from training, showing a plan, journal, measurement of quality and reliability rates.

The assessor will look for the trainer demonstrating that they:

1.   Link together different behaviours without deterioration in the quality of each individual behaviour.
2.   Build a chain of individual behaviours that is commenced with a single cue.

3. Cue collections of behaviours that individually are not given a click, other verbal feedback or signal and only reinforced at the end.

4. Collect data and analyse the learning and results.

5. Free shape using targets and cues whilst not overtly directing the learning.

6. Show the process of linking behaviours by altering the timing of the reinforcement.

Tests can be taken by video in any format. Details on the website:

www.learningaboutdogs.com

Appendix B

EXPLODING BEHAVIOUR

SHAPING PROGRESS MAPS

Before you begin to shape, sketch an idea of the possible route the dogs will take and the steps you will break it down into.

It helps if you have a clear picture in your mind of how you see the dog completing the behaviour(s) and the variations the dog may need to take. The key step is working out the opening point, and assessing what skills the dog may need to start at all.

This is a sample of my pick-up shaping plan, which allows for this dog, who already likes to run around with soft toys, to progress onto a dumbbell. Most of our toys end up as "skins", when the stuffing has been removed. In fact other skinned toys make for excellent stuffing and I believe the hedgehog contains a dead duck and a chipmunk.

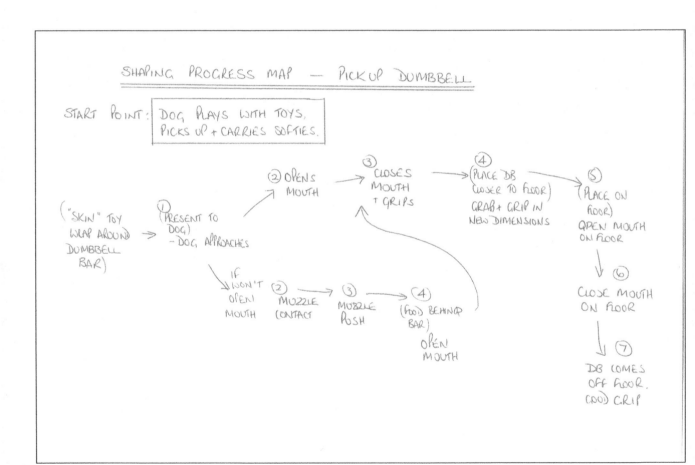

EXPLODING GROUPS OF BEHAVIOURS

To practise and develop your ability to examine the individual behaviours in groups, make a list of the behaviours you would teach in these groups.

1. Sort out which steps can be achieved with free shaping and make a shaping progress map for the possible steps to the behaviour.

2. Make a note of the individual behaviours that would make a merge and the clusters you may teach along with the cues (possible solutions over next page)

1. Dog running out to drop between 4 markers

2. Dog to collect article and deliver to named location

3. Dog to safely approach children playing and interact

4. Dog to run to bed, pull up blanket and go to sleep

possible solutions over next page

1. DOG RUNNING OUT TO DROP BETWEEN 4 MARKERS

Prior behaviour: lay down from standing at distance of 20 foot (merged behaviour of distance and the drop)

    a.   shape dog to target mat

             dog to stand on mat on cue "mat"

             build distance to 20 foot, dog to run out on cue

    b.   place mat between four markers

             dog to confidently run to mat in new location on new cue "markers"

             reduce size of markers

    c.   randomly cue variety of behaviours on arrival, which includes "drop".

progress map for shaping dog to mat

prior skills: none

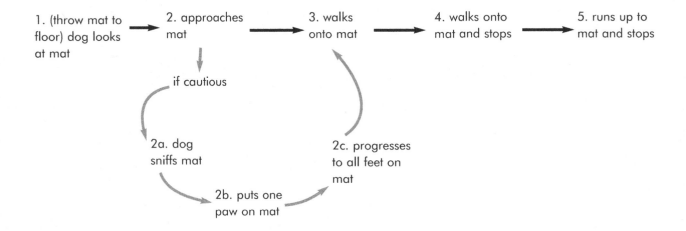

2. DOG TO COLLECT ARTICLE AND DELIVER TO NAMED LOCATION

Prior behaviour: Retrieve a range of articles

a.   dog to retrieve named article

      dog to identify article from amongst other articles, some searching

      dog to reject other articles when named cue given

      dog to collect from out of sight as well

b.   dog to go to named location

      use mat or other target to get "go to" skill

      increase distance, perhaps out of sight

      change cue from mat to location cue

c.   dog to place article on cue

      dog to stop at location

      dog to drop or place article onto target

d.   sequence behaviours on direct cues

3. DOG TO APPROACH CHILDREN PLAYING

Prior behaviour: asssessment test for handling and petting from children

This is a merged behaviour for a child friendly dog

a. dog to sit on cue

      cue changed to visual recognition of children

b. dog to maintain sit:

      whilst children talking and laughing

      with high excitement levels of children

      whilst you: wave hands, jump up and down

            hug with unsympathetic hands

      multiple handling from known adults

c. merge behaviours

4. DOG TO RUN TO BED, PULL UP BLANKET AND GO TO SLEEP

a.   shape sleepy behaviour either:

> fall flat on side with head on floor
>
> lie with paw over face

b.   retrieve shaped for short pull

> transfer retrieve to lying down flat position
>
> increase distance until dog retrieves from over back legs and pulls towards front legs
>
> transfer article used for short pull and attach to blanket
>
> dog to pull blanket whilst lying down

c.   dog to go to bed

> dog to lie down in bed for settled position

d.   sequence for self running chain: (with blanket already in position on end of bed)

"Are you ready for bed?"	dog goes to bed
"settle"	dog lies with hips rolled
"chilly?"	dog pulls blanket over to shoulders
"tired?"	dog lies with head on pillow or foot over face

SHAPING CHALLENGES

These are some of the behaviours we have trained my dogs and our class dogs to do. The more basic exercises are covered in Foundation and Novice Books

Some ideas are offered for the shaping progress map, but not all dogs will progress in the same way. Keeping an open mind and allowing the dogs to solve the puzzles is essential.

BEHAVIOUR	SHAPING MAP	Final Cue Verbal	Final Cue Signal
Stay at a distance	Toss food to distance, when dog ready and looking	Out	Hand up
On my left side	Lured for precision	Tight	Hand on hip
On my right side	Lured for precision	Leg	Hand on hip
In front of me, facing me	As concentration training, with exercise to move hips in line	In Front	Hands together at waist
Trotting	With target stick, placed for type of movement, head up or head level.	Trot	Hand out guiding
Run	Target stick, moving fast to encourage canter or ball play	Fast	=
Walking backwards	Shape step by step, looking for back feet moving fluently	Walk back	=
Side steps, with front and back feet in line	By moving the in front location	Gee to the right	=
		Hah to the left	=
Go around me in a circle	Target stick followed around you, you stand still and take the target around	Go round	=

Turn in a small circle clockwise	Target stick	Spin	=
Turn in a small circle anti clockwise	Target stick	Turn	=
Rotate with front feet fixed	Shaped from standing on a stool	Turn or Spin + stool	=
Weave through my legs	Target stick to cue under the leg, then change to other leg	Through	going under bent knee
Take a bow	Shaped from head nod, through bending elbows, until resting on floor	Bend	
Beg	With target stick when in a square sit	Begging?	
Dead doggie, lying flat on one side or with feet in air	Shaped from the settle down, to drop head, shift elbows and fall over. Feet in air from paw to hand cue	Fall over	
Wipe your face	Captured from after dinner wiping face with feet (and on sofa)	Tired?	
Roll over	Shaped from dead doggie, roll brings dog upside down and over takes dog out and upright	Roll + Over	Hand to signal which way
Jump in the air on the spot nose or feet up	Target stick for nose, click for spring in air	Pop	High 5 hand
Jump in air as a lamb, spine level	Side jump the dog over a low bar, fade bar	Spring	
Look away from trainer in fixed direction	Target stick against a wall, click when dog looks before movemenr towards it	Look	
Place front paw on precise spot	Using rubber ring large enough to take paw in the centre	Polo	
Go around object	Shaped with flank close to object	Go round + object	

Stand on object	Shaped from paws on stool to large object	On the box
Collect the shopping and place it in the basket	Shape retrieve objects by individual name	" ***** "
	Place object into basket	Basket
	Carry basket	Shopping

SHAPING CHALLENGES

These are ideas for you to play around with - no answers here!

1. Teach the dog to walk backwards around a post or marker

2. Teach the dog to push a ball or toy between two goal posts from any direction

3. Teach the dog to march on the spot

4. Teach the dog 10 objects on specific verbal cues

5. Teach the dog to climb a ladder

Appendix C

FORMS:

STRENGTH OF A BEHAVIOUR

REINFORCEMENT VALUES

MICRO SHAPING REINFORCEMENT RATE

TEST: | **STRENGTH OF BEHAVIOUR**

DOG: [   ]   **AGE:** [   ]

LOCATION: [   ]

Reward ratio   1:1

TEST BEHAVIOUR(S):						
1						
2						
3						
4						
5						
6						
7						
8						
9						
10						
% AT STRENGTH 3:						

BEHAVIOUR:

0 = DOES NOT HAPPEN

1 = WEAK IN BOTH MEMORY AND PHYSICAL SKILL

2 = WEAK IN EITHER MEMORY OR PHYSICAL SKILL

3 = STRONG IN BOTH MEMORY AND PHYSICAL SKILL

TEST: | **REINFORCER VALUE**

DOG: | [   ]   **AGE:** | [   ]

LOCATION: | [   ]

TEST BEHAVIOUR: | [   ]

Behaviour	**A**	**B**	**C**	
Reward ratio	1:1	1:0	0:1	
1				
2				
3				
4				
5				
6				
7				
8				
9				
10				
Highest Valued Reinforcer				

BEHAVIOUR:

0 = DOES NOT HAPPEN

1 = WEAK IN BOTH MEMORY AND PHYSICAL SKILL

2 = WEAK IN EITHER MEMORY OR PHYSICAL SKILL

3 = STRONG IN BOTH MEMORY AND PHYSICAL SKILL

TEST: | **MICRO SHAPING REINFORCEMENT RATE**

DOG: | **AGE:**

LOCATION:

BEHAVIOUR:

1 minute sessions	1	2	3	4	5	6
1						
2						
3						
4						
5						
6						
7						
8						
9						
10						
11						
12						
13						
14						
15						
16						
17						
18						
19						
20						
21						
22						
23						
24						
25						
NO. OF BEHAVIOURS OFFERED (A)						
NO. OF CLICKS PER MINUTE (B)						
RATE OF SUCCESS %						

- = NO BEHAVIOUR
/ = BEHAVIOUR
✓ = CLICKED BEHAVIOUR
✗ = MISSED THE CLICK BEHAVIOUR

RATE OF SUCCESS = B DIVIDED BY A MULTIPLIED BY 100

$B/_A \times 100 = \%$

Made in the USA
Monee, IL
18 May 2021